DARK CHOCOLATE

DARK
CHOCOLATE

A GUIDE TO ARTISAN CHOCOLATIERS

Steve Huyton

PELEUS PRESS

CONTENTS

AN ENDURING PASSION THROUGH THE AGES

The chocolate industry is on the threshold of a new reawakening. An old industry, steeped in tradition, it holds mystical beliefs in an ingredient, cacao, that dates back to a time before modern man.

From those who first discovered the edible qualities of the cacao bean and to this day, many believe that *Theobroma cacao*, or, 'food of the gods', nourishes the soul.

Cacao itself has been on a long journey, from its ancient beginnings in a world full of spiritual beliefs in the Americas, before moving across the globe to Europe but also being established on cacao farms around the equator, and then finding itself in the industrial Victorian age of machinery. And here it is in the present, with the modern artisan chocolate maker who combines spirituality and emotional well-being to handcraft these amazing chocolates for you to enjoy. The true awakening has been to the ever-present qualities of the unique flavours of age-old cacao, and thus dark chocolate.

How can a food be so desired, so longed for, so needed in our lives? You may choose to eat chocolate for its medicinal values or because you just love the deep notes of caramel, plum and berry.

Or you prefer to enjoy single-origin chocolate for its complexity and depth, or perhaps it's a love of those 'feel good' emotions that make you all dreamy as you munch on a quality chocolate bar. The modern chocolate maker combines all these emotions into our products, with an ever-changing understanding of what food is. We, the chocolate makers, are the creators of emotion.

What we so carefully craft are not just products. They become part of us, an extension of ourselves, they are what we believe: chocolate as unique and wonderful as the artisans creating them. Chocolate making is a true craft that gives me much pleasure. But there's a responsibility for nurturing something so precious and remaining true to the core values of the beans. It's the very essence of chocolate.

Origin Chocolate is a purist's delight, with each chocolate being as exotic as the place of its birth. There's an evolution in taste with each bar being unique, with flavours that are familiar but never quite the same.

I am the creator of the food of the gods. I am a chocolate maker.

Matt Chimenti, Founder, Origin Chocolate

MY DARK AWAKENING

I have always appreciated chocolate, but once having tasted my first true artisan dark chocolate bar, I was blown away by the texture, complexity of flavours, aromas and richness. It was different to any chocolate I had ever encountered. I was both intoxicated and intrigued, and determined to learn about bean-to-bar high-cacao-content chocolate.

The artisan chocolate industry is experiencing tremendous growth globally. Craft chocolatiers, driven by flavour, are creating incredible products while remaining true to their ideals, and finding new aficionados. For who can resist a quality, hand-crafted product that is literally 'the food of the gods'?

These craft producers all have one thing in common: they are all dedicated to the traditional art of creating chocolate using the bean-to-bar process, while respecting its integral unique flavour.

Highlighting this dedication is the packaging used by each artisan, whether it be an eye-catching design or more neutral in colour but made from recyclable paper. And there are often surprises contained on the inside of the wrapping. Many chocolatiers use distinctive customised moulds, adding personality and recognisability to their products.

Within the industry I have discovered so many passionate chocolate makers who will go to extraordinary lengths to manufacture an exquisite product. Their enthusiasm for the delicious treat they craft is infectious. And the highest accolade for a chocolatier is that the consumer truly appreciates the result.

This is only a selection of dark chocolate artisans and their creations from around the globe. We know that chocolate targets the pleasure receptors in our brains, producing a feeling of well-being. With this thought in mind, I encourage you to investigate the handcrafted dark chocolate possibilities out there. After all, it's guilt-free chocolate, an affordable taste of luxury and it's good for you. Welcome to the dark side!

Steve Huyton

I THINK ALL OF US WHO LIKE CHOCOLATE (AND WE ARE QUITE A FEW), CAN MAKE THE WORLD BETTER BY CHOOSING A CHOCOLATE THAT IS NOT ONLY GOOD FOR US BUT ALSO DOES GOOD FOR THE EARTH AND THE PEOPLE WHO CULTIVATED CACAO.

Jenny Berg, CO-FOUNDER, VINTAGE PLANTATIONS

A DARK BACKGROUND

WHAT IS DARK CHOCOLATE?

Dark chocolate can be defined as chocolate that is made without dairy products, and has a high cocoa content (from say 60% to 100%). It may also (but not always) consist of only two ingredients: cocoa (namely cocoa mass and cocoa butter) and some form of sweetener.

The artisan manufacturing process of dark chocolate is fascinating, and has been compared to that of wine making. Just like grapes, the flavour of cacao beans can vary dramatically depending on weather and soil conditions, topography as well as how the bean is processed (fermentation times, drying times, long or slow roastings, percentage of cacao used, and so on). Essentially this means that the flavour, intensity, aroma and texture is different for every batch of chocolate.

WHAT IS IN DARK CHOCOLATE?

CACAO BEANS

Theobroma cacao, the 'food of the gods', only grows within 20 degrees north or south of the equator, largely in South America, Central America, West Africa and Southeast Asia. Cacao has been cultivated for thousands of years in Mexico, Central and South America.

For many years, it was thought that there were three broad types of cacao. We now know that there are many more varieties, and new ones are still being discovered. Common names you may encounter:

Criollo These are the premium cacao beans, and most desired, attracting a higher price. They are harder to grow, but offer delicious and intriguing flavour notes. Criollo beans make up less than 5% of cacao production.

Trinitario These cacao beans are widely used in the chocolate industry, and have a robust flavour. Trinitario is a hybrid of Criollo and Forastero.

Forastero These are widely used, and often blended with premium beans by small companies.

HEIRLOOM

Heirloom is an all-encompassing description, used in different ways for marketing purposes. It may refer to an indigenous variety of cacao, or an old subspecies of one of the three common types. Or it may refer to a very old tree, handed down through generations of a family. It may also mean that the strain of cacao has been around since before industrialised agriculture. Heirloom beans have been referred to as the diamonds of cacao, endowed with historic, cultural, botanical and most importantly, flavour values. Their unique flavour profile attracts higher market prices.

Arriba Possibly the most well-known of the heirloom varieties, this type is found largely in Ecuador, and dates back more than 5,000 years.

Amelonado A varietal of the Forastero cacao.

Wild cacao Wild cacao can be defined as that which grows in the jungle, and is often gathered by local indigenous communities. With its unique flavours derived from its wild upbringing, wild-harvested cacao is in great demand by craft producers. These beans are often smaller than their more cultivated relations.

CUPUAÇU

A close relative of the cacao bean, *Theobroma grandiflorum,* known as *cupuaçu* in Brazil, is attracting interest for its culinary possibilities, including crafting chocolate with a colour akin to milk chocolate.

SWEETENER AND FLAVOURINGS

Dark chocolate will often (but not always) include some form of sweetener, usually cane sugar, but sometimes coconut blossom sugar, Stevia or other alternatives. The sweetener counterbalances the bitterness of the cacao, and makes the taste more pleasurable.

Additional flavourings such as vanilla, peppermint essence, chilli or more varied options like lavender or fennel may be included as a flavour enhancement.

HOW DO YOU MAKE DARK CHOCOLATE?

In this book, we discuss bean-to-bar, tree-to-bar and raw chocolate makers. The techniques employed are all different and therefore yield varied results.

By the time you unwrap an artisan chocolate bar, the chocolate has already been through many steps. Cacao pods are harvested by hand, and the beans are extracted, ready for fermentation. After this, the beans are dried, then sorted for shipping. The bean-to-bar chocolatier roasts the beans to bring out their flavour. Then, the beans are cracked and winnowed, to remove the shells and reveal the cacao nib. The nibs are ground to produce the cocoa liquor, or cocoa mass, before being conched and then tempered. Conching results in evenly distributed cacao butter for a smooth texture. Tempering results in a quality chocolate with a shiny finish and a firm snap. Lastly, the chocolate is poured into moulds, and then wrapped (often by hand), ready for distribution. Raw chocolate is made from unroasted cacao beans, which advocates claim results in higher levels of antioxidants and a more natural taste.

WHY IS DARK CHOCOLATE GOOD FOR US AND THE PLANET?

HEALTH BENEFITS

For years people have eaten mass produced chocolate confectionery that is composed of mostly fat and refined sugar. However, dairy-free dark chocolate with its relatively high cacao content contains many benefits, including the chocolate taste! Plus its slightly bitter and rich taste means you are less likely to overindulge.

Some people are put off by the bitterness of dark chocolate with its high-cacao content. With dark chocolate, any sweetener is there to balance the bitterness, and there will be a significantly lesser percentage than commercial chocolates. A good dark chocolate should be perfectly balanced, and not too bitter. Milk chocolate includes dairy products, which bind with the flavonoids and renders them inaccessible. With dark chocolate, the cacao flavours are able to speak for themselves. We recommend not being put off by the bitterness of the cacao, but instead encourage beginners to persevere, and concentrate on the myriad flavours from the rich variety of handcrafted chocolate bars.

Cacao, and therefore dark chocolate, with its high cacao content, both contain a high level of antioxidants, minerals (magnesium, sulphur, zinc, calcium and manganese) and vitamins A, C and E. Chocolate even has theobromine, which can help to reduce blood pressure, a hint of caffeine to decrease fatigue, and the cocoa butter fat is cholesterol-free. Many of the artisan chocolate bars are organic, vegan, gluten-free, and sometimes even sugar-free.

Cacao beans contain polyphenols, an antioxidant shown to reduce stress levels. They also contain molecules that activate the pleasure receptors in the brain, and create serotonin, which produces feelings of well-being and relaxation. So there's a scientific reason behind chocolate being a great pick-me-up on down days.

FAIRLY TRADED

The brands featured in this book all have high production values, with ethical pricing for the cacao beans used to handcraft their chocolate.

SUSTAINABLE

The chocolate makers included all have a concern for the well-being of their farmers as well as the environment in which the cacao trees grow. Many are working with their supplier farmers to encourage organic and sustainable farming, and working to restore the land and its biodiversity. Maintaining old-growth trees also provides important habitat for native endangered species.

FLAVOUR

The careful balancing of the flavour profiles of the beans with the necessary sweetness results in a rich, silky smooth treat, and a luxurious indulgence that leaves you feeling happier. This balancing act is in itself an art form, albeit a dark one, perfected by the artisan chocolatiers, after much testing.

In addition, many producers are experimenting with innovative and unique flavour and texture combinations, and new ingredients to open up a wealth of novel taste options. Indeed, the only limit to flavour possibilities is the imagination of the chocolatier as they all seek to raise the bar. Expect the unexpected when chocolate is paired with sea salt flakes, or chilli, or perhaps even some dried mushroom and seaweed, or ancient grains like quinoa or amaranth.

A GUIDE TO TASTING CHOCOLATE

Enjoying fine dark chocolate can be compared to wine tasting, and even some of the terminology is the same. Each chocolate bar contains its own unique flavour profiles from the cacao bean, which has been exposed to many variables such as topography, weather, soil conditions, post-harvesting processes and, of course, what sort of variety it is.

Here are a few hints to get the most out of the chocolate tasting experience, and hopefully the most enjoyment out of your dark chocolate experience.

PREPARATION

Firstly, try to have a quiet environment, allowing you to concentrate on the detection of the flavours. Cleanse your palate before you begin with a piece of apple or bread, and have warm water available to sip between tasting if you are trying multiple chocolates. Most importantly, allow the chocolate to rest at room temperature. A cold chocolate does not give up its flavours.

APPEARANCE

Enjoy the process of unwrapping the chocolate from its beautiful packaging, revealing the beauty within. First, admire the overall rich colour of the chocolate. Is the colour more black or reddish brown? Even though you may think of chocolate as being a monochrome colour, careful inspection will render the tints of colour discernible. (Tip: try holding the chocolate at different angles to see the full range of colours.) Does the chocolate have a glossy finish? Quality chocolate will have a shiny, glossy appearance. Is the edge of the chocolate smooth with an even colour, or is it coarse and grainy in appearance, a sign of a lesser quality bar? Observe the chocolate surface to see that it is free of defects such as white marks (known as bloom), and air bubbles or an uneven surface, which result when the chocolate settles poorly after moulding.

SNAP

The chocolate should make a clear 'snap' when broken. If there is no audible 'snap', the chocolate may be too warm, or may have been incorrectly tempered.

AROMA

What aromas can you detect when you break the chocolate bar? Each artisan chocolate batch is unique, but common aromas may include tobacco, malt, fruits, warm spices and woody notes. Try to discern if the aroma is faint or intense, fruity or floral, earthy or nutty.

MOUTHFEEL AND MELT

Take that first bite, letting the chocolate melt slowly in your mouth, releasing its complexity of flavours. Taking it slowly allows the cocoa butter to be evenly distributed. The melt of the chocolate is all-important, and should result in a silky and sensuous sensation. The texture itself in the mouth should be creamy and smooth, with no graininess, dryness or stickiness.

TASTE

You might notice flavours such as toffee, butterscotch, liquorice and coffee. Concentrate on how the flavour evolves from beginning to middle and end. Bite and chew the chocolate on a second tasting to release other individual aromas and flavours. Be aware of the acidity, bitterness, sweetness and astringency of the chocolate. A good chocolate will result in a well-balanced mix of flavours, with just enough acidity, for example, to enhance fruity flavours rather than overpower it.

FLAVOUR TIME

The best quality chocolates will have a long, lingering finish. Try to see how long the flavour lasts.

ARTISAN CHOCOLATIERS

ALTER ECO

Alter Eco was established 16 years ago in France by Tristan Lecomte. In 2005 Edouard Rollet and Mathieu Senard opened offices in San Francisco, United States, and launched the brand in North America while Ilse Keijzer started an office in Sydney, Australia, for the distribution of the brand in Australia and New Zealand. The company is committed to making wholesome, healthy food that is carefully crafted to enrich people's lives, entwining the founders' principles with the determination to use only the best ingredients, sourced ethically. Pioneers of full-circle sustainability, the brand only works with small-scale farmers who grow all the organic and non-GMO ingredients that go into its tantalising range of chocolate bars. The fair trade agreements produce benefits for everyone involved in the process.

Try the addictive and indulgent Salted Burnt Caramel for its intense flavour and deep salty crunch.

GLUTEN FREE | SOY FREE | NON-GMO

70%
COCOA

ALTER ECO®

DARK SALTED
BURNT
CARAMEL

ORGANIC CHOCOLATE

deep salty crunch

USDA
ORGANIC

FAIRTRADE

NET WT. 2.82 OZ 80G

SALTED BURNT CARAMEL

RAW CANE SUGAR, CREAM AND BUTTER ARE SIMMERED
TO THE BRINK OF BURNT FOR A MASTERFUL CARAMEL CRUNCH
BEFORE BEING COVERED IN DARK ECUADORIAN CHOCOLATE, AND SPRINKLED
WITH FLEUR DE SEL DE GUÉRANDE FOR A MALTY CRUNCHY FINISH.

BLACKOUT

A SERIOUSLY DARK BAR FOR THOSE WHO ARE SERIOUS ABOUT CHOCOLATE. AT 85% CACAO, THIS INTENSE CONCOCTION BALANCES FRUITY DEPTH WITH A ROUND, SMOOTH, CREAMY FINISH.

QUINOA

PUFFED QUINOA LENDS ITS SATISFYING CRUNCH AND NUTTY FLAVOUR TO MALTY ECUADORIAN CHOCOLATE. RAW CANE SUGAR AND MADAGASCAN VANILLA FINISH A CLASSIC RECIPE WITH PURE FLAVOUR.

MINT

SILKY SMOOTH ECUADORIAN CACAO IS CONTRASTED WITH A REFRESHING GRITTY CRUNCH OF PEPPERMINT ESSENCE CRYSTALS AND A MELLOWING TOUCH OF MADAGASCAN VANILLA.

SALT & MALT

FLEUR DE SEL DE GUÉRANDE MEETS BOLD, DEEP ECUADORIAN CHOCOLATE. THE EFFECT IS SWEET YET SALTY, SMOOTH YET CRISPY, NOSTALGIC YET ENTIRELY NEW.

SALTED ALMONDS

ROASTY-TOASTY ALMONDS SWIM IN DEEP, DARK ECUADORIAN CHOCOLATE, WITH A SPRINKLING OF COVETED FLEUR DE SEL DE GUÉRANDE TO HEIGHTEN EACH AND EVERY FLAVOUR.

SEA SALT

A GENEROUS STIRRING OF FLEUR DE SEL DE GUÉRANDE ADDS A SUBTLE, MOUTH-WATERING CRUNCH TO THE DEPTH AND MALTINESS OF ECUADORIAN CACAO. EVERY BITE IS THE PERFECT BALANCE OF SALTY AND DARKLY SWEET.

AMMA CHOCOLATE
— BRAZIL —

AMMA Chocolate, a premium, organic bean-to-bar brand in Brazil, has recently opened a franchise in Byron Bay, Australia, tapping into the region's reputation for excellent gourmet food. The business is underpinned by the desire to create a superior product using the finest ingredients like organic cacao, raw sugar and cocoa butter, while respecting the environment and population. The brand's mission is also to preserve and reforest the Atlantic Forest of South Bahia and create a more sustainable socio-economic climate within the region. The range of chocolate bars on offer provides numerous exciting flavour combinations.

All are absolutely delicious but the cupuaçu (*Theobroma grandiflorum*; a close relative of the cacao tree) is outstanding with its unique flavour and texture.

CUPUAÇU

MADE USING THE BEANS OF THE TANGY
CUPUAÇU. THIS BAR PRESENTS UNIQUE
AND INTENSE EARTHY FLAVOURS,
WALNUT NOTES AND A BUTTERY
TEXTURE. ITS APPEARANCE IS LIGHTER,
DUE TO THE LIGHT COLOURING OF
THE *CUPUAÇU*.

QAH'WA

AN EXPLOSIVE COMBINATION OF HARMONIOUS ALKALOIDS (CAFFEINE AND THEOBROMINE), THIS BAR HAS A CRUNCHY TEXTURE AND OVERALL ESPRESSO FLAVOUR.

AROEIRA

THE CHEEKINESS OF THE FRUIT DISGUISED
IN THE CHARM OF THE AROMATIC PINK PEPPER
RESULTS IN A SLIGHTLY SWEET FLAVOUR
AND A SOPHISTICATED CHOCOLATE WITH
A UNIQUE PERSONALITY.

FLOR DO MAR

A PERFECT BALANCE OF CHOCOLATE INTENSITY
AND DELICATE SEA SALT CRYSTALS. THE CONTRAST
BETWEEN THE OPPOSING SWEET AND SALTY
FLAVOURS IS FORGOTTEN AT THE FIRST BITE.

GULAH MERAH

MADE FROM GULAH MERAH (ALSO KNOWN
AS COCONUT PALM SUGAR) RATHER THAN CANE
SUGAR, THIS CHOCOLATE HAS A CITRUS FLAVOUR,
WITH A SLIGHTLY BITTER TASTE
AND MILD ACIDITY.

NIBIRUS

THE INTENSITY OF THE CACAO NIBS, CRACKLING
THROUGH THE FRUITY CHOCOLATE, GIVES A
CRUNCHY TEXTURE, WITH A SOUR CHERRY FLAVOUR
AND A FLORAL AFTERTASTE.

ANTIDOTE CHOCOLATE

— USA —

Antidote truly provides a delicious, decadent yet guilt-free chocolate cure for the stresses of modern life. The creative powerhouse behind the brand is a dynamic Austrian lady called Red Thalhammer, with an extensive background in design. In 2009 she decided to make the leap and establish her own boutique chocolate company, using sustainable and equitable practices to create a power chocolate. After a lengthy process of product development, Red elected to use only the finest Ecuadorian Arriba Nacional cacao beans. These are combined with ingredients like real chunks of fruits and spices, including mango, ginger, fennel, cayenne, cardamom, to produce an enticing and innovative range of dark chocolate bars.

For a special occasion, choose the magnificent and surprising Lavender + Red Salt bar.

LAVENDER + RED SALT

LAVENDER FLOWERS MINGLE WITH GRAINS
OF EARTHY RED-ALAEA SALT ON DARK CHOCOLATE
OF 84% SLOW-ROASTED CACAO, GIVING A POTENT
AND FLORAL TASTE EXPLOSION.

MANGO + JUNIPER

SOPHISTICATED AND SEXY, THIS DARK
CHOCOLATE MIXES TOGETHER TIDBITS OF DRIED
MANGO WITH CRUSHED JUNIPER BERRIES,
SEDUCING WITH THEIR DIZZYING PINE PERFUME,
TO PRODUCE A RICH AND AROMATIC BAR.

CRAFTING FLAVOURS IS LIKE CREATING ART OR COMPOSING MUSIC. THE PROCESS NEEDS
DRAMA, HIGH POINTS AND LOW POINTS, AND A BIT OF TENSION WOVEN THROUGHOUT.
WHEN THAT ALL COMES TOGETHER, YOU HAVE A SYMPHONY MADE OF CHOCOLATE.

Red Thalhammer, FOUNDER, ANTIDOTE CHOCOLATE

BANANA + CAYENNE

THE CRISPY DRIED ECUADORIAN BANANAS
MATCH THE PEPPERY CAYENNE TO PROVIDE
A DARK AND SPICY FINISH, ALL ON A BED
OF DARK CHOCOLATE.

ROSE SALT + LEMON

ROSE SALT FROM THE ANDES IS PAIRED
WITH TANGY LEMON ZEST ON A BED OF
DARK CHOCOLATE, CREATING A SUBTLE
AND DELICATE FLAVOUR.

ALMOND + FENNEL

CRUNCHY ALMONDS ARE COMPLEMENTED BY
CHEEKY SWEET-LIQUORICE FENNEL SEEDS ON DARK
CHOCOLATE OF SLOW-ROASTED CACAO TO GIVE A
RICH AND SAVOURY TASTING EXPERIENCE.

COFFEE + CARDAMOM

AROMATIC ARABICA COFFEE AND MINTY CARDAMOM
ARE TRIUMPHANT ON RICH, DARK CHOCOLATE. THE
COFFEE, GROWN IN THE MOUNTAIN SHADE OF THE
LOJA REGION IN ECUADOR, HAS BEEN SPECIFICALLY
SELECTED TO COMPLETE THIS TASTE TRIFECTA.

BAHEN & CO
— AUSTRALIA —

Bahen & Co is a boutique brand in Margaret River, Western Australia. At the helm is former winemaker Josh Bahen, who has focused on the art of making fine chocolate, employing a traditional approach using stone-ground chocolate. Over the years he has established solid fair trade agreements with farmers. Distinctively, Bahen & Co uses vintage machinery (an antique winnower, a 1930s Barth Sirocco Ball Roaster and a 1910 Guitard melangeur) to achieve a super-fine texture. As well as crafting bars with extraordinary flavours, the company also produces delicious single-origin bars containing only two ingredients (cacao beans and raw cane sugar). The beautifully designed packaging is designed to take people on a journey, and the patterns are inspired by the exotic places the founders visited to source beans.

Don't miss the decadent Madagascar bar, made with heirloom beans, and with a delightful citrus note.

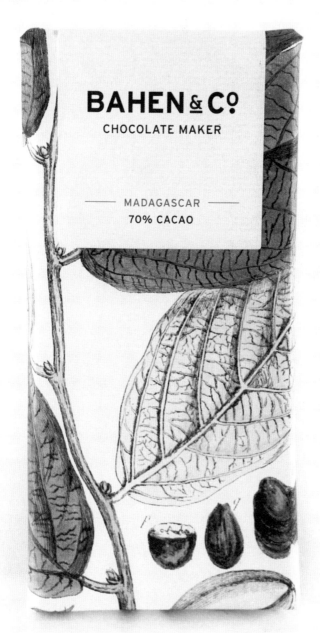

MADAGASCAR

ORIGINALLY ESTABLISHED IN THE SAMBIRANO VALLEY IN THE 1920S, THIS RARE HEIRLOOM FARM PRODUCES CACAO BEANS WITH A LIVELY FLAVOUR OF CITRUS, AND RUM AND RAISIN.

ALMOND & SEA SALT

ALMONDS, SLOW-ROASTED WITH BAHEN'S OWN OLIVE OIL, ARE COVERED WITH
HOUSE BLEND CHOCOLATE, BEFORE BEING FINISHED WITH HANDHARVESTED SEA
SALT, GIVING A SWEET YET SALTY EXPERIENCE WITH ADDED CRUNCH.

BRAZIL

MADE FROM CACAO BEANS FROM A PLANTATION ONCE LOST IN THE JUNGLE, THIS CHOCOLATE EXUDES MULLED WINE, FRUIT CAKE AND BOLD CHOCOLATE NOTES.

CRACKED COFFEE

THIS BAR CONTAINS LIGHTLY ROASTED ARABICA COFFEE BEANS, CRACKED OVER BOLD BRAZILIAN CHOCOLATE; BOTH BEAN TYPES ARE SINGLE-ORIGIN.

HOUSE BLEND 70%

A SELECTION OF SINGLE-PLANTATION CACAO BEANS ARE STONE GROUND TO PRODUCE A COMPLEX CHOCOLATE.

HOUSE BLEND 80%

SINGLE-ORIGIN CACAO BEANS ARE BLENDED TOGETHER TO CREATE A PERFECT DARKER CHOCOLATE MIX.

CACAOKEN

Cacaoken is an exclusive bean-to-bar chocolate brand located in Iizuka, Fukuoka, Japan. The name derives from 'cacao laboratory' in Japanese. Discerning food fanatic Yukari Nakano is the creative force behind the business. Yukari's passion for the industry is totally contagious. All the products are fastidiously handcrafted using the finest cacao beans (sourced largely from Vietnam, where Cacaoken has established a farm and research lab). Yukari experiments with the length of fermentation for the beans, to deliver varied flavours. The petite chocolate bars pack an intense taste into their small volume. The attention to detail and quality has resulted in many awards and accolades for Cacaoken.

Try both the Black Haiti and Black India varieties to experience their intense flavour profiles.

BLACK HAITI

THE CACAO BEANS FROM HAITI GIVE A
GENTLE AND DELICATE FLAVOUR TO THE
CHOCOLATE, WITH AROMAS OF HAZELNUTS,
HONEY AND WOOD.

カカオ研究所
cacaoken

BLACK
HAITI
80% CACAO

BLACK VIETNAM

THESE CACAO BEANS GIVE A DISTINCTIVE
FRESHNESS AND A TOUCH OF ACIDITY, WITH A
SWEETNESS AT THE FINISH. THE CHOCOLATE HAS
HERBAL, LIME AND PASSION FRUIT AROMAS.

BLACK BLEND

THIS CHOCOLATE, MADE FROM VIETNAMESE AND
GHANAIAN BEANS, HAS AROMAS OF ROASTED
PEANUTS AND RED BERRIES,
WITH SOUR FRUIT NOTES.

DEEP

PRODUCED USING A LONG FERMENTATION PROCESS,
THESE VIETNAMESE CACAO BEANS GIVE THE
CHOCOLATE AROMAS OF DRIED PRUNES,
RED BERRIES AND AN EARTHY NOTE.

LIGHT

PRODUCED USING A SHORT FERMENTATION
PROCESS, THE SAME VIETNAMESE CACAO BEANS
GIVE A MORE FLORAL AROMA, WITH HINTS OF
LEMON ZEST AND PASSION FRUIT.

BLACK INDIA

MADE FROM TRINITARIO CACAO BEANS FROM INDIA, THE CHOCOLATE PRODUCES A
SPICY AROMA, WITH HINTS OF CARDAMOM AND MINT.

CAONI CHOCOLATE

— ECUADOR —

Caoni Chocolate is a small chocolate-making enterprise located in the heart of Ecuador. The business was founded by three enterprising business partners over a decade ago. They were inspired by the hard work of the Ecuadorian cacao farmers and, in particular, their harvest of exceptionally fine cacao beans. This incentivised them to add value to this incredible organic product and make a range of small-batch chocolate bars. The rest is history and now the company has won several awards for its sensational single-origin bars. Caoni's chocolatiers respect the unique aromas and textures of the cacao, following hundreds of years of tradition.

The robust yet elegant flavour of the exquisite Los Rios bar speaks to these years of tradition and excellence.

IT'S SATISFYING TO SEE PEOPLE CHOOSE YOUR CHOCOLATE FROM AMONG ANY
OTHER BRAND, BECAUSE YOU KNOW YOU'RE DOING SOMETHING RIGHT. SEEING
OTHER PEOPLE EAT OUR CHOCOLATE IS A SIGN OF SUPPORT OF OUR COUNTRY
AND CACAO FARMERS, IT'S ECUADORIAN PRIDE.

Barbara Brauer, CAONI CHOCOLATE

LOS RIOS

THIS CHOCOLATE REVEALS AN INTENSE COCOA
FLAVOUR WITH HINTS OF NUTS AND TOFFEE, SHOWING
THE CLASSIC ELEGANCE THAT IS CHARACTERISTIC OF
THIS ECUADORIAN REGION.

GOLDEN BERRY

THE DISTINCTIVE FLAVOUR OF GOLDEN BERRIES, ALSO KNOWN AS CAPE GOOSEBERRIES, BLENDS PERFECTLY WITH THE SMOOTH AROMAS OF THIS CHOCOLATE, SOURCED FROM THE ECUADORIAN AMAZON REGION.

NIBS

THE SMOOTH AMAZONIC FLAVOURS OF THE CACAO BEANS GROWN IN THE JUNGLE PERFECTLY COMBINE WITH THE STRONG AROMATIC FLAVOURS OF OVEN-ROASTED ARRIBA CACAO NIBS.

MACADAMIA

THE SPECIALLY TOASTED MACADAMIA NUTS CREATE AN INCREDIBLE TASTE AND TEXTURE, COMBINING PERFECTLY WITH THE DARK CHOCOLATE.

MANABI

THIS BAR REFLECTS THE TYPICAL CHARACTERISTICS OF THE MANABI CACAO BEANS; SWEET, CREAMY, SMOOTH WITH A DISTINCTIVE FRUITY AROMA. THIS CHOCOLATE IS IDEAL FOR BEGINNERS IN THE CHOCOLATE ADVENTURE.

PASSION FRUIT

CRAFTED FROM CACAO BEANS FROM THE ECUADORIAN AMAZON REGION, ITS FLAVOUR REFLECTS THE BIODIVERSITY OF THE JUNGLE AND COMBINES PERFECTLY WITH THE NATURAL TROPICAL FLAVOUR OF THE PASSION FRUIT.

CHALEUR B CHOCOLAT

— CANADA —

This boutique family-run company is situated on the edge of the Chaleur Bay in Quebec, Canada, and called, appropriately enough, Chaleur B Chocolat. Dany Marquis is the owner, and has run a successful coffee-roasting business since 2005. After a trip to Europe in 2007 he became interested in the art of chocolate making, becoming in due course one of Canada's most innovative chocolatiers. The lengthy seven day process starts with cacao beans that are ground, winnowed and tempered for the ultimate bean-to-bar experience. Even though the bars are diminutive in size and handmade in small batches, they are each made with love, patience, dedication and, as a result, they taste extraordinary.

Be seduced by the refined flavour and blackcurrant aromas of the 80% Kallari bar.

KALLARI

DARK REFRESHING AROMAS OF BLACKCURRANT WITH NOTES OF GREEN PEPPERS AND MINT ON A SWEET VANILLA FINISH. THIS BAR IS NAMED AFTER AN ECUADORIAN PRODUCER ASSOCIATION THAT PURCHASES CACAO BEANS AND OTHER INGREDIENTS FOR A FAIR PRICE FROM THE LOCAL FARMERS.

NO 1 LUMO

THIS CHOCOLATE IS BRIGHT AND BRILLIANT, WITH A DOMINANCE OF CITRUS, AND SLIGHTLY ACIDIC WITH HINTS OF CANDIED FRUIT.

NO 2 RUGA

WITH ONE BITE, YOU GET HINTS OF RED FRUIT, PLUM, AND THEN YOU NOTICE SOME TANNIN, BEFORE A FINAL SWEET FINISH.

NO 3 SPICO

THIS BAR CONTAINS AROMAS OF SPICE, FIG AND TOBACCO, AND A VERY COCOA FINISH. A GOOD EXAMPLE OF THE EFFECT OF A LONG AND INTENSE FERMENTATION OF THE BEANS.

NO 4 MOLCO

THE AROMAS OF GRAPES, DRIED FRUITS AND NUTS ALL WORK TOGETHER TO GIVE THIS CHOCOLATE A PLEASANT AND COMFORTING SWEETNESS.

ZORZAL

THERE'S A REAL EXPLOSION OF APRICOT, HONEY, AND CARAMELISED NUTS. IT TASTES LIKE JAM IN A CHOCOLATE BAR. THE CACAO COMES FROM THE RESERVA ZORZAL BIRD SANCTUARY IN THE DOMINICAN REPUBLIC.

FABRICATION ARTISANALE

ENTRE LES MAINS LE
DEVOUEMENT COLLECTIF
METTRA D'EXPLORER ET
LES MEILLEURS TERROIRS
MONDE, EN PASSANT PAR
TEUR, JUSQU'À NOTRE
DE LA FÈVE DE CACAO
ABLETTE DE CHOCOLAT.

DING IN YOUR HANDS THE,
COLLECTIVE DEDICATION
LOW YOU TO EXPLORE AND
EST COCOA TERROIRS IN
OING FROM THE FARMERS,
KSHOP, FROM THE COCOA
YOUR CHOCOLATE BAR.

DCRAFTED
OCOLATE

EURB.COM

CHALEUR B CHOCOLAT

·CRÉATEUR DE CHOCOLAT·

CHOCOLAT
ARTISANAL
HANDCRAFTED
CHOCOLATE

COLLECTION MICRO-LOT

75% ZORZAL

RÉPUBLIQUE DOMINICAINE / DOMINICAN REPUBLIC

40g

NOIX · MIEL · CARAMEL · ABRICOT
WALNUT · HONEY · CARAMEL · APRICOT

CHOCOLAT MADAGASCAR

— UK/MADAGASCAR —

With offices in the UK and Madagascar, this producer has received many awards for its quality pure chocolate. What makes this company unique is the fine flavour of the Sambirano cacao and the natural techniques used to craft the chocolate fresh at its source, providing a huge benefit to the local economy. The terrain and climate of the land result in beans with unique flavour profiles. Chocolat Madagascar crafts the cacao beans into chocolate in days rather than months, and with no chemical processing (alkalisation), the flavours and flavonoids are preserved for optimum taste and health benefits. In addition, the cacao is grown in the rainforest, thereby ensuring a haven for Madagascar's unique flora and fauna.

To experience the unique flavours of the Madagascar cacao, try both the Domaine Mava and Domaine Vohibinany bars.

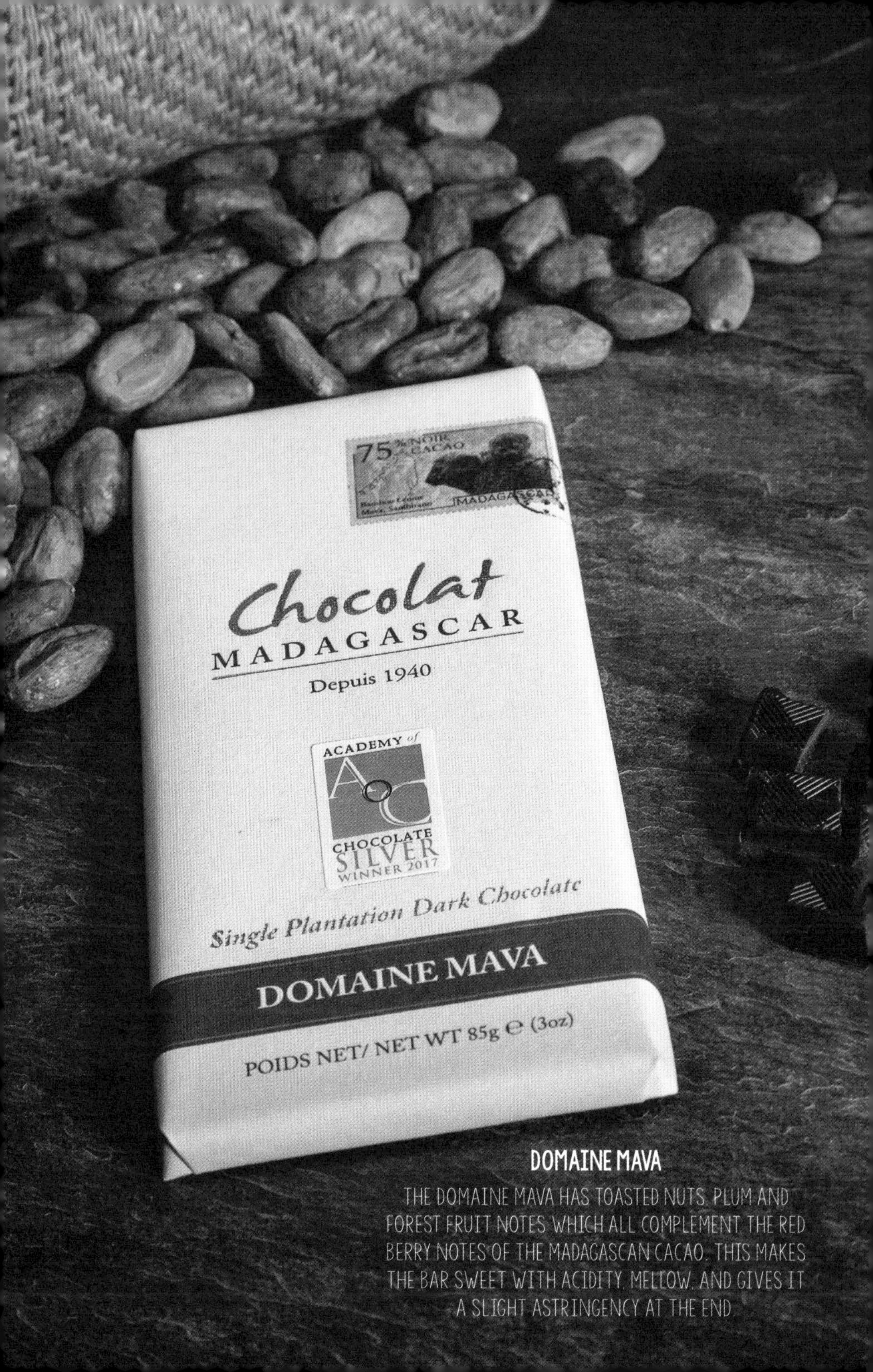

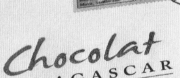

75% NOIR CACAO
MADAGASCAR
Chocolat
MADAGASCAR
Depuis 1940
ACADEMY of
CHOCOLATE
SILVER
WINNER 2017
Single Plantation Dark Chocolate
DOMAINE MAVA
POIDS NET/ NET WT 85g ℮ (3oz)

DOMAINE MAVA

THE DOMAINE MAVA HAS TOASTED NUTS, PLUM AND FOREST FRUIT NOTES WHICH ALL COMPLEMENT THE RED BERRY NOTES OF THE MADAGASCAN CACAO. THIS MAKES THE BAR SWEET WITH ACIDITY, MELLOW, AND GIVES IT A SLIGHT ASTRINGENCY AT THE END.

DOMAINE VOHIBINANY

THIS IS A SINGLE-PLANTATION BAR CRAFTED FROM VERY RARE CACAO BEANS, CAPTURING THE DELICATE NUTTY FLAVOURS AND PRODUCING AN OVERALL MELLOW CHOCOLATE TASTE WITH CLASSIC RED BERRY FRUITS, AND A LONG FINISH.

65%

RICH FLAVOURS OF FOREST FRUITS, RAISINS, HINTS OF HONEY AND ORANGE FROM THE FINE AND RARE TERROIR CRU OF CRIOLLO-TRINITARIO CACAO GROWN IN THE SAMBIRANO RAINFORESTS.

70%

A VERY FINE SEED-TO-TREE-
TO-BAR CHOCOLATE WITH
SENSATIONS OF RED BERRIES,
HINTS OF PEPPER, AND A MULLED
WINE FINISH.

85%

THE FLAVOUR AND AROMATIC
MARRIAGE FROM THE CAREFULLY
FERMENTED AND ROASTED CACAO
BRINGS OUT A CONCERT OF
RED BERRIES, CITRUS, RAISINS,
NUTS AND SPICES IN PERFECT
HARMONY.

100%

THE PUREST CHOCOLATE BAR
WITH ONLY ONE INGREDIENT,
THIS AWARD-WINNING
CHOCOLATE HAS A SMOOTH,
BUTTERY TEXTURE AND SWEET
FRUITINESS. THE HIGH
CACAO BUTTER PERCENTAGE
COMPLEMENTS THE INTENSE
COCOA KICK.

CHOW CACAO
— AUSTRALIA —

Chow Cacao is a specialist microbrand situated in the seaside location of Byron Bay, Australia. Owners Trudy and Wil are passionate about healthy natural foods, which is why all their fair trade, vegan, organic, preservative-free raw chocolate contains only the finest ingredients like cacao from Peru and coconut palm sugar from Indonesia. The couple also wants to promote the benefits of cacao, which contains magnesium, antioxidants and iron. Within a short amount of time the company has rapidly expanded from local markets to the shelves of many Australian supermarkets. This is the result of the couple's hard work and an uncompromising attention to quality. Even though each bar is small, the taste is exceptionally rich and intense.

The clear winner is the exceptionally decadent Peanut Butter Slab.

PEANUT BUTTER SLAB

THE TASTE OF WICKED WITHOUT THE FEELS. COMBINING
RAW CACAO AND HOMEMADE PEANUT BUTTER.

CREAMY COCONUT MILK

PLAYING THE HARD GUY WITH THE DARK
CHOCOLATE CONTENT, THIS BAR SURPRISES
WITH A CREAMY COCONUT-MILK CHOCOLATE.

SMOOTH PURE DARK

PURE AND POWERFUL, THIS IS CHOCOLATE IN ITS TRUEST FORM,
LOADED WITH MINERALS AND ANTIOXIDANTS THAT, IF ENJOYED IN
MODERATION, CAN BE THE KIND OF CHOCOLATE YOU EAT EVERY DAY.

DARK CRUNCHY MINT

THIS MEMORABLE TASTE
CLASSIC PACKS A PUNCH,
STIMULATING YOUR TASTEBUDS
IN THE FRESHEST WAY
POSSIBLE, WITH CACAO NIBS
INCLUDED FOR THE ADDITIONAL
CRUNCH.

SOUR CHERRY COCONUT

THIS BAR CONTAINS A ZESTY RIGHT AND A
SWEET LEFT, WITH A TROPICAL TWIST.

DARK ORANGE ALMOND

THIS BAR CONTAINS A FRUITY
NOTE OF ORANGE WITH THE NUTTY
CREAMINESS OF ALMOND.

CLAUDIO CORALLO

— SÃO TOMÉ AND PRÍNCIPE —

Even among the diverse stories of the chocolate makers, Claudio Corallo's story is unusual. At the age of 23, he relocated from Italy to establish a new life in Zaire, Africa, before political instability forced him to move to São Tomé and Príncipe. Here he purchased a rundown cocoa plantation containing Forastero cacao trees, direct descendants of the trees brought from Brazil by the Portuguese in 1819. Claudio makes his living as a simple farmer producing organic cacao, Liberica coffee and pepper on several plantations. This enables him to make one of the freshest chocolates available on the market. Claudio's primary objective is for all his loyal customers to experience a true tree-to-bar experience.

If you love intense, robust flavours then trying the UBRIC 1 is a prerequisite.

MY FAVOURITE ONE IS UBRIC. I LOVE TO HAVE IT RIGHT AFTER DINNER AND EVERY TIME IT GIVES ME GOOSEBUMPS. WHEN ITS TEMPERATURE IS AROUND 28°C (82°F) THE TENDERNESS IS INCOMPARABLE AND THE CHOCOLATE HARMONISES PERFECTLY WITH THE BODY. ITS ENERGY VIVIFIES ME EVEN 24 HOURS LATER.

Claudio Corallo, FOUNDER, CLAUDIO CORALLO

100% CACAO

THIS BAR PROVES THAT GOOD CHOCOLATE DOES NOT HAVE TO BE BITTER. THE POWERFUL IMPACT OF THE TANGY FLAVOUR AND TEXTURE IS FOLLOWED BY A SWEET, LINGERING AFTERTASTE.

ESFERAS

THESE EXQUISITE CRYSTALLISED GINGER SPHERES PRODUCE FRESH AROMAS OF GINGER ON THE PALATE SUCCEEDED BY THE RICH AND POWERFUL TASTE OF THE EARTHY CHOCOLATE.

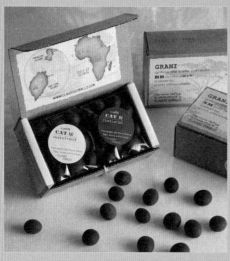

GRANI

GRANI SHOWCASES HOW THE DIFFERENCE IN PROCESSING AFFECTS THE SAME VARIETY OF COFFEE BEAN, BEFORE BEING COVERED IN CHOCOLATE.

LIBERICA

A BLEND OF 70% CHOCOLATE WITH VENERABLE AND EXTRAORDINARY LIBERICA COFFEE BEANS, ROASTED IN THREE DIFFERENT WAYS TO BRING OUT THEIR AMAZING FLAVOUR.

ROASTED CACAO BEANS

THIS SELECTION OF BEANS BRINGS THE REAL TASTE OF PLANTATION CHOCOLATE TO LIFE. TO EAT THE BEAN, HOLD IT BETWEEN YOUR THUMB AND INDEX FINGER. PUSH IT DOWN LIGHTLY ONTO A HARD SURFACE, AND DISCARD THE BITTER ROOT AND THE SHELL.

CLONAKILTY CHOCOLATE

— IRELAND —

In a small rural town in Canada, a young Allison Roberts dreamed about becoming a successful chocolatier. This vision was realised many years later and she has now established a successful chocolate brand, not in Canada but in Ireland. As well as selling a range of delicious treats locally the company also distributes its bean-to-bar products worldwide. Combining fair trade Ghanaian cacao beans with natural coconut sugar ensures the absolute perfect flavour while at the same time paying homage to the mystical and humble cacao bean. Allison employs a highly experimental approach to this art, and is always trying out new flavours and textures. All of its sustainably produced packaging is 100% biodegradable.

A standout is the tasty Chai Chilli bar, with its broad mix of spices punctuating the sharpness of the cacao.

CHAI CHILLI

SWEET, AROMATIC AND LIGHT WITH DARK UNDERTONES, THE FIVE SPICES HIT ONE BY
ONE, LEAVING A MOUTHWATERING AFTERTASTE.

100% PURE

FULL-BODIED CHOCOLATE WITH DRY, RED FRUIT AND NUTTY, SHARP MID-TONES AND SMOOTH EDGES; A VERY ACCESSIBLE 100% BAR.

ORANGE

A DEEP AND SIMPLE CHOCOLATE, CONTAINING A RICH LIQUOR, ROUGH WITH A SILKY ORANGE EDGE.

WILD WEST SALTY

AT FIRST DRY, THEN EXCITING WITH A SLIGHTLY TEXTURED SAVOURY EDGE AND EARTHY TONES, A RICH CHOCOLATE THAT MELTS INTO SPIKES ON THE TASTE BUDS.

SERIOUSLY MINTED

COOL, REFRESHING CHOCOLATE, WITH HINTS OF RED FRUIT, AND A TEXTURE THAT MELTS TO BECOME CREAMY AND RICH.

DECADENT DARK

THIS SUGAR-FREE BAR IS COOL AND BRIGHT ON FIRST IMPRESSION, MELTING TO BECOME RICH AND VELVETY DARK WITH DISTINCT EARTHY WEST AFRICA NOTES OF RED FRUIT AND AROMATIC SPICE.

WE LIKE TO KEEP IT SIMPLE. CHOCOLATE IS GOOD. IT TASTES GOOD.

WE MAKE CHOCOLATE THAT IS GOOD FOR US — OUR BODIES AND OUR COMMUNITIES.

Allison Roberts, FOUNDER, CLONAKILTY CHOCOLATE

CONSCIOUS CHOCOLATE

— UK —

Conscious Chocolate is a small independent brand located in England. Since 2004, the company has produced premium quality, organic products that are sold worldwide. Primary markets include the UK, Ireland, continental Europe and the Middle East. All of its vegan, raw chocolate is handmade (from ethically sourced ingredients) and individually wrapped in its own kitchens to ensure the highest quality-control levels. Ultimately, this ensures that customers receive a delicious treat free of gluten, dairy, soy and refined sugar every time. As an added bonus, all of its packaging is environmentally friendly (biodegradable and compostable).

For those seeking a mellow yet luxurious experience, try the delightfully textured Goji & Coconut bar.

❀ · ❀ · ❀ · ❀

GOJI & COCONUT

ORGANIC GOJI BERRIES AND COCONUT CHIPS GIVE THIS BAR
A DELIGHTFULLY CRUNCHY TEXTURE.

THE DARK SIDE

WITH 85% CACAO SOLIDS, THIS IS A
SUPER RICH DARK CHOCOLATE BAR, WITH
INTENSE FLAVOURS.

ESSENTIAL ORANGE

THE HARMONIOUS BLEND OF ORANGE AND
TANGERINE OILS IN THIS BAR IS BOTH
COMFORTING AND UPLIFTING TO THE
SENSES, GIVING SWEET AND CITRUSY
FLAVOUR NOTES.

MINT HINT

THIS BAR IS AS CREAMY AS IT IS MINTY,
LEAVING YOU WITH A CLEAN,
REFRESHING FINISH.

LOVE POTION NO 9

FLORAL AROMAS ARE FOLLOWED BY A
SENSUOUS FLORAL TASTE, REMINISCENT
OF TURKISH DELIGHT, ALL ENROBED IN
RICH DARK CHOCOLATE

NUTTY ONE

GENEROUS AMOUNTS OF
FOUR DIFFERENT, COARSELY
CHOPPED ORGANIC NUTS
ARE BLENDED WITH RICH,
RAW CHOCOLATE FOR AN
INCREDIBLE TEXTURE.

EARTH LOAF

— INDIA —

Earth Loaf is a chocolate manufacturer located in Mysore, India, dedicated to making premier gourmet raw chocolate. All the single-origin bars are handcrafted in very small batches to achieve the absolute maximum quality, and to showcase the distinctive terroir and flavour of south Indian cacao. The company was established by David Belo and Angelika Anangnostou who both share a passion for quality and nutritious food. Earth Loaf produces a raw chocolate range with intense and robust flavours, combining exhilarating ingredients such as chilli, ginger, coffee and mango with the finest cacao beans. As a perfect finishing touch, all of its products are presented in locally made, beautiful handprinted packaging.

It is difficult to go past the enticing combination of Smoked Salt & Almond.

SMOKED SALT & ALMOND

DARK CHOCOLATE GARNISHED WITH HOMEMADE SMOKED SALT, A TOUCH OF PALMRYA SUGAR AND ORGANIC ALMONDS FROM KASHMIR PROVIDES THE PERFECT BALANCE OF SALT AND SWEETLY RICH CACAO.

72%

THIS SINGLE-ESTATE CHOCOLATE IS SWEETENED WITH COCONUT SUGAR AND HAS A ROBUST FLAVOUR PROFILE WITH PROMINENT ACIDITY, FRUITINESS, HINTS OF RAISINS AND SUBTLE UMAMI AND TOBACCO.

GONDHORAJ & APRICOT

THE PALATE SALIVATES WITH THE SWEET, TANGY FLAVOURS OF GONDHORAJ AND APRICOT, CARRIED BY THE FLORAL LIME AND ENDING WITH DEEP CACAO NOTES.

COCONUT, GINGER & GONDHORAJ

THE MILD ACIDITY OF THE CHOCOLATE INTERPLAY WITH MANGO GINGER FROM THE ANDAMAN ISLAN WITH A HINT OF FLORAL GONDHORAJ LEMON AN CREAMY COCONUT.

MANGO, RED CAPSICUM & CHILI

SWEET, FRAGRANT, YET SLIGHTLY TART MANGOES ARE SET AGAINST SAVOURY BUT SWEET RED PEPPERS, MARRIED WITH FRESH VANILLA, BEFORE A TOUCH OF RED CHILLI ADDS A SUBTLE KICK TO THE FINISH.

TOKAI COFFEE & PINEAPPLE

A SUBTLE INTERTWINING OF NUTTY COFFEE AND FRUITY CACAO BEANS IS GIVEN AN ETHEREAL LIFT BY THE SWEET AND TANGY PINEAPPLE AND FRESH VANILLA.

HIMALAYAN FRUIT & NUT

CHOCK-FULL OF ORGANIC APRICOTS, ALMONDS, RAISINS AND APPLES AND COVERED WITH ORGANIC ARTISAN DARK CHOCOLATE.

EQUAL EXCHANGE

— USA —

Founded over 30 years ago, Equal Exchange is a worker-owned co-operative with a simple mission: building long-term mutually beneficial partnerships with organised farmer groups that have similar values. Beginning this work with coffee in Nicaragua, the co-operative has since expanded to work with farmers who grow cocoa, tea, bananas, and other fairly traded foods.

Using only fairly traded ingredients from small farmer co-ops around the globe, Equal Exchange has built up a tantalising range of organic chocolate.

Awaken your taste buds with the unusual and surprising tangy taste sensation of Lemon Ginger with Black Pepper bar.

LEMON GINGER

SWEET AND CITRUSY, THE SURPRISING COMBINATION OF LEMON AND GINGER WITH DARK CHOCOLATE IS WELL BALANCED AND REFRESHING. THE BAR FINISHES WITH A HINT OF BLACK PEPPER, ROUNDING OUT THE SPICINESS OF THE GINGER.

VERY DARK

THIS 71% CACAO BAR PROVIDES A DELICIOUS, INDULGENT AND INTENSE FULL-BODIED DARK CHOCOLATE EXPERIENCE.

EXTREME DARK

MADE WITH 88% CACAO, THIS BAR HAS DELICIOUS AND ROBUST TASTE PROFILES, BEFORE MELTING INTO A DARK FUDGY RICHNESS.

CARAMEL

CRUNCHY CARAMEL BITS SERVE AS THE PERFECT COMPLEMENT TO MOUTHWATERING SEA SALT CRYSTALS AND BRING OUT THE COMPLEX FLAVOURS OF THE SMOOTH, FRUITY CHOCOLATE.

PANAMA

THIS DARK BAR IS PERFECTLY BALANCED TO ALLOW THE TRUE CHOCOLATE FLAVOUR OF THE PANAMANIAN BEANS TO SHINE.

MINT

THE DELICATE MINT CRUNCH PROVIDES A WONDERFUL COMPLEMENT TO THE CREAMY, DEEP CHOCOLATE; AN IDEAL BALANCE OF RICH, DARK CHOCOLATE AND LIGHT, REFRESHING MINT.

FU WAN CHOCOLATE

— TAIWAN —

Fu Wan Chocolate is a small artisan brand based in Taiwan. The business was established by executive chef Warren Hsu who is committed to handcrafting a superb range of bean-to-bar products. Over the last few years the company has won several awards and has established sustainable fair trade agreements with local farmers. Warren showcases the distinct flavour of the Taiwanese cacao, and pairs it with surprising ingredients. As well as producing single-origin bars, Fu Wan Chocolate also produces novel flavours like apricot kernel and quinoa.

However, nothing really compares to the chef's special, a delicious experimental bar, which contains shrimp, pomodori (sun-dried tomato), paprika, cayenne pepper, and maple sugar.

62% NIBS

IN ADDITION TO THE AROMAS OF THE
TAIWANESE CHOCOLATE, THE INCLUSION
OF THE NIBS AFFORDS EVEN MORE NOTES:
THE SOURNESS OF TROPICAL FRUIT, AND
AN EVEN MORE PRONOUNCED CHOCOLATE
AND NUTTY FLAVOUR.

62%

THE FIRST TASTE ESTABLISHES HONEY-
BUTTER COOKIE NOTES, TOFFEE, MOLASSES
AND THE SUBTLE SOURNESS OF PINEAPPLE
AND GREEN MANGO. THE EXPERIENCE
CONTINUES WITH A HINT OF ALMOND,
BEFORE FINISHING ON A CARAMELISED
COFFEE NOTE.

APRICOT KERNEL

THE ECUADORIAN CHOCOLATE BESTOWS
NUTTY NOTES, ACCOMPANIED BY
THE FLORAL HONEY FLAVOUR OF THE
ROASTED APRICOT KERNEL (A KIND OF
CHINESE ALMOND).

QUINOA

THE QUINOA AND ELEGANT RICE NOTES COME TOGETHER WITH THE TAIWANESE DARK CHOCOLATE, WHICH IS FULL OF HONEY BISCUIT AND ALMOND BROWNIE FLAVOURS.

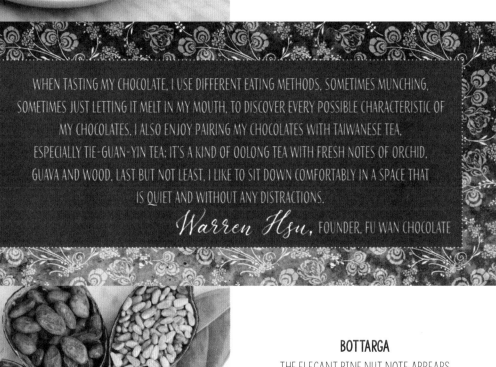

WHEN TASTING MY CHOCOLATE, I USE DIFFERENT EATING METHODS, SOMETIMES MUNCHING, SOMETIMES JUST LETTING IT MELT IN MY MOUTH, TO DISCOVER EVERY POSSIBLE CHARACTERISTIC OF MY CHOCOLATES. I ALSO ENJOY PAIRING MY CHOCOLATES WITH TAIWANESE TEA, ESPECIALLY TIE-GUAN-YIN TEA: IT'S A KIND OF OOLONG TEA WITH FRESH NOTES OF ORCHID, GUAVA AND WOOD. LAST BUT NOT LEAST, I LIKE TO SIT DOWN COMFORTABLY IN A SPACE THAT IS QUIET AND WITHOUT ANY DISTRACTIONS.

Warren Hsu, FOUNDER, FU WAN CHOCOLATE

BOTTARGA

THE ELEGANT PINE NUT NOTE APPEARS FIRST, FOLLOWED BY THE BONITO NOTES OF THE SALTED FISH ROE. THE ECUADORAN DARK CHOCOLATE PROVIDES WELL-ROUNDED FLAVOURS OF NUT, HONEY AND COCONUT. AT THE END IS BOTTARGA AND UMAMI, FINISHING THE EXPERIENCE WITH A CLEAN BONITO NOTE.

GOODNOW FARMS CHOCOLATE

— USA —

While visiting a vintage shop in Los Angeles, Tom and Monica Rogan had a taste epiphany that changed their perception of chocolate, and their lives. Subsequently this led them on a journey to discover some of the world's finest cacao beans. These are incorporated into chocolate bars, which are produced on the 225-year-old farm, in Sudbury, Massachusetts, United States. The couple source cacao beans from a single farm or region to enable them to discover and highlight the distinct flavour characteristics. The company has developed ethical relationships with all the farmers and suppliers it uses. Tom and Monica state "that great chocolate is true to the bean".

Be utterly seduced by the sophisticated texture and flavour of the Esmeraldas bar.

ESMERALDAS

MADE FROM THE INCREDIBLY FLAVOURFUL NACIONAL HYBRID CACAO BEAN,
THIS CHOCOLATE HAS OVERTONES OF BERRY JAM, WITH EXTREMELY LOW ACIDITY,
AND MELLOW ASTRINGENCY. IT ENDS ON A LONG, NUTTY, SATISFYING FINISH.

ALMENDRA BLANCA

A SHORT, LIGHT ROAST HIGHLIGHTS THE NATURALLY BRIGHT, FRUITY
FLAVOUR OF THE ALMENDRA BLANCA BEAN, GIVING RISE TO SPICY
NOTES WITH A TOUCH OF LIQUORICE.

ASOCHIVITE

THE CHOCOLATE MADE FROM THIS BEAN HAS A DELIGHTFULLY BRIGHT, SHARP AND FRUITY FLAVOUR, WITH LIGHT ACIDITY AND A MELLOW, DARK-FRUIT FINISH.

EL CARMEN

A CUSTOM DRYING TECHNIQUE IS USED TO PERFECTLY HIGHLIGHT THE BRIGHT FLAVOURS OF THIS BEAN, REVEALING NOTES OF DRIED RAISINS, BURNT CARAMEL AND ROASTED BLACK TREACLE.

NICALIZO

THE COMPLEX FLAVOURS IN THIS LIMITED EDITION BAR INCLUDE GRAPES AND RAISINS, WITH A SLIGHT WOODY AFTERTASTE.

UCAYALI

A HERBAL AND FLORAL BAR, THIS CHOCOLATE HAS NOTES OF LEMON VERBENA AND FIG, WITH A TOUCH OF HONEY.

GREEN & BLACK'S

— UK —

Green & Black's was originally established in 1991 by Craig Sams and Josephine Fairley. With backgrounds in organic food and journalism, the duo combined forces and created a progressive fair trade brand. The couple were early pioneers when they introduced chocolate with a high cocoa content to the mainstream market, and also led the way in using organic farming and fair trade. Green & Black's proved its doubters wrong as its Maya Gold bar was awarded the Worldaware Business Award in 1994. Subsequently the company was taken over by Cadbury and now has a strong retail presence in regions around the globe. However, it still remains true to the ideals of the founders.

The well-rounded, smooth Dark 85% bar is a deserved favourite for good reason.

85%

HIGH LEVELS OF CACAO ARE MIXED WITH SUGAR AND
ORGANIC VANILLA TO SEPARATE THE BITTERNESS AND THE
ACIDITY, RESULTING IN AN ALMOST SAVOURY NOTE WITH
A PERFECTLY BALANCED TASTE AND FLAVOUR PROFILE.

DARK **85%**

GREEN
&BLACK'S
ORGANIC

Dark Chocolate
very dark, very smooth,
softened with Madagascan vanilla

85% Cocoa

® e 100g

Per 6 Pieces (20g)
520 kJ
125 kcal
6%*
Per 100g
2610 kJ
630 kcal

70%

A RICH COCOA TASTE COMES FROM THE TRINITARIO CACAO BEANS, AND A COMPLEX, AROMATIC FLAVOUR PROFILE THAT INCLUDES NUTTY TONES, ROASTED COFFEE AND BITTER CHERRY.

PIONEERING CHANGE

"The British will never eat dark chocolate." That's what supermarkets told me when I first showed them Green & Black's in 1991. Little did they know that the chocolate industry was at the dawn of a new era. Not only has appreciation for chocolate changed since those early days, so has the way chocolate is grown and sourced, helping to transform the lives of cacao farmers and their families.

When Josephine and I founded Green & Black's, the chocolate market was dominated by a handful of large chocolate manufacturers. Nobody traded directly with cacao farmers. Direct and fair trade was unheard of. We also had to develop our own sources of organic cacao, by building strong and lasting relationships with cacao farmers. Today, our biggest source of gratification comes from seeing how the principles we applied to sourcing cacao are now becoming universal across the entire chocolate industry.

Craig Sams, CO-FOUNDER, GREEN & BLACK'S

GINGER

AT FIRST, THE FIERY, SPICY, CRYSTALLISED GINGER STAYS LOCKED AWAY INSIDE THE 60% DARK CHOCOLATE. BUT, AS IT MELTS, A HIT OF GINGER FINDS ITS WAY TO YOUR PALATE.

SEA SALT

DELICATE FLAKES OF ANGLESEY SEA SALT OFFER A SURPRISING AND DELICIOUS CONTRAST TO THE SOFT CHARACTER OF THE CHOCOLATE, CULMINATING IN A DELICATE CRUNCH AND TRULY MOREISH FLAVOUR.

ROASTED ALMOND

MEDITERRANEAN ALMONDS, RO WITH THEIR SKINS ON FOR A INTENSE FLAVOUR, LEND THEIR C TEXTURE TO THE RICH YET SM CHOCOLATE TASTE.

MINT

THIS BAR DELIVERS A REFRESHING MINT FLAVOUR WHICH COMPLEMENTS THE SWEET AND DELICATE CHARACTER OF THIS GHANAIAN CHOCOLATE, BALANCED WITH MADAGASCAN VANILLA.

JASPER & MYRTLE

— AUSTRALIA —

Jasper & Myrtle is a small family-owned chocolate company located in Australia's capital city, Canberra. Owners Li Peng and Peter visited a chocolatier while on holiday, and were enamoured by the chocolate-making process. The visit sparked a decision to launch their own chocolate business. In a short amount of time the brand has won multiple awards for its delicious and experimental bean-to-bar gourmet products. The company sources the finest quality cacao from around the world, including Peru and Papua New Guinea, and combines them with flavourful ingredients. Recently it has won a huge order for its sublime chocolate with a national retailer in Australia.

Feeling adventurous? Try the sensational Himalayan Rock Salt & Wakame bar.

HIMALAYAN ROCK SALT & WAKAME

THIS IS A UNIQUE AWARD-WINNING CHOCOLATE, WITH COMPLEX LAYERS OF FLAVOURS. IT ALSO HAS A NICE COMBINATION OF SWEET, SOUR, VANILLA AND UMAMI.

GINGER & COCONUT

CHUNKS OF GINGER ARE ENTWINED WITH MOIST FLAKES OF COCONUT, RESULTING IN A SPICY, TEXTURED AND RICH CHOCOLATE EXPERIENCE.

PERUVIAN 66%

MADE WITH THE RARE CRIOLLO BEAN FROM PERU, THIS SINGLE-ORIGIN CHOCOLATE IS DELICATE AND CLEAN TASTING. SILKY AND SMOOTH IN TEXTURE, IT HAS WELL-BALANCED FRUIT NOTES WITH NO BITTERNESS.

ESPRESSO

CANBERRA ARTISAN ROASTED
COFFEE BEANS IN THIS CHOCOLATE
GIVE A GOOD HIT OF COFFEE,
WHICH MAKES THIS A PERFECT
AFTER-DINNER CHOCOLATE.

PNG 66%

MADE WITH THE TRINITARIO
BEAN FROM PAPUA NEW GUINEA,
THIS IS A ROBUST CHOCOLATE,
WITH AN INTENSE, EARTHY AND
FULL-BODIED FLAVOUR.

SPICED RUM

THIS IS A SOPHISTICATED
CHOCOLATE THAT LINGERS ON THE
PALATE, AND IS CHARACTERISED
BY SUBTLETY AND SILKINESS,
AND FLAVOURED WITH FRUIT
AND SPICES SOAKED IN
AUSTRALIAN BUNDABERG RUM.

MADE WITH RAW LOVE

— AUSTRALIA —

Made with Raw Love is an innovative chocolate manufacturer located near Byron Bay, Australia. Holistic nutritionist Tahlia and photographer/artist Scott joined forces to create an exceptionally exciting and experimental microbrand, one that shares their love of chocolate and good health. All the chocolate bars (made from a compound of raw cacao from Peru and Ecuador and organic coconut oil) are handcrafted in very small batches. At this stage the couple adds a range of extraordinary ingredients like Matcha green tea and bee pollen as well as Australian native bush plants such as Kakadu plum or lemon myrtle. These flavours might sound eclectic but in fact the taste combinations are exciting.

The standout is the highly adventurous Immuni Shroom bar with its complex flavours.

♡ · · ♡ · · ♡ · · ♡

IMMUNI SHROOM

A COMPLEX FLAVOUR WORTHY OF TRUE ROYALTY, WITH THE KING AND QUEEN OF MEDICINAL MUSHROOMS ADDING THEIR DELICIOUS EARTHY UNDERTONES WHEN MATCHED WITH VANILLA AND CINNAMON FOR JUST A LITTLE SPICE.

BRAIN LOVE

LEMON MYRTLE AND FINGER LIME ARE
UPLIFTING AND ZESTY, A PERFECT MATCH
FOR THE EFFECTS OF LIONS MANE AND
GOTU KOLA ON THE BRAIN.

WE ENJOY OUR CHOCOLATE ANY TIME OF DAY, BUT PARTICULARLY A PIECE AFTER DINNER. TO GET THAT MELT-IN-YOUR-MOUTH MOMENT, KEEP THE CHOCOLATE AT ROOM TEMPERATURE, OR FOR THAT CRISP SHARP BREAK, POP IT IN THE FRIDGE. THE BEAUTY ABOUT BEING THE CHOCOLATIERS IS THAT WE HAVE ALL FLAVOURS OF CHOCOLATE AVAILABLE TO US AND CAN PICK WHATEVER FLAVOUR RESONATES FOR US AT AT ANY GIVEN TIME. WE TEND TO ALWAYS GO BACK TO THE IMMUNI SHROOM AS ONE OF OUR TOP FAVOURITES. WE CREATE EACH FLAVOUR WITH THE INTENTION TO ENRICH YOUR BODY AND SOUL.

Tahlia and Scott, FOUNDERS, MADE WITH RAW LOVE

COCO NILLA

THE ADDITION OF COCONUT ADDS TEXTURE
AND CREAMINESS TO ONE OF OUR MOST
TREASURED FLAVOURS AND AROMAS:
VANILLA.

MINT BIOTIC CRISP

THE FINEST PEPPERMINT OIL, THE PERFECT AMOUNT OF CRISP RESULT IN A REFRESHING AND REVITALISING CHOCOLATE PACKAGE, WITH A BALANCING BLEND OF PREBIOTIC AND PROBIOTIC FOR OPTIMAL GUT HEALTH.

BUSH FOOD

THE FINEST CACAO FROM PERU AND ECUADOR IS RICH IN FLAVOUR BUT VELVETY SMOOTH. COMBINED WITH THE SHERBETY TONES OF RIBERRY AND KAKADU PLUM, TWO DISTINCTLY FLAVOURED AUSTRALIAN BUSH FOODS.

OPEN HEART

FRANKINCENSE IS BOTH HEALING AND DECADENT, WITH AN ALMOST INDESCRIBABLE FLAVOUR THAT HAS EXCITED THE SENSES THROUGHOUT THE AGES. DEHYDRATED BLUEBERRIES (FULL OF ANTIOXIDANTS) PROVIDE A WONDERFUL TEXTURE AND FLAVOUR.

MALAGOS CHOCOLATE

— PHILIPPINES —

Malagos Chocolate first began in 2003 when Roberto and Charita Puentespina leased a farm with cacao trees. It took many years of nurturing the neglected Trinitario cacao trees before the brand could be launched in 2013. The business has since grown significantly and has won many international awards. A recently opened chocolate museum explores the process of making tree-to-bar chocolate, and the history of Philippino chocolate. In 2017 the farm's cacao beans were recognised as being among the world's best 50 (from 166 cacao beans samples received from 40 countries) by the prestigious Cocoa Excellence Programme in France.

If you love bold, strong flavours then you won't be able to resist sampling the 85% dark bar.

85%

A SLOW LINGERING MELT-
IN-THE-MOUTH EXPERIENCE
THAT RELEASES COMPLEX
AND INTENSE COCOA
FLAVOURS. THIS CHOCOLATE
STRIKES THE PERFECT
BALANCE CONSIDERING THE
HIGH COCOA CONTENT.

Malagos
chocolate

85% Dark
Chocolate

SINGLE-ORIGIN DAVAO

All Natural
Made from Tree to Bar

Net Weight 100g (3.53oz)

STRONG AND INTENSE CACAO TONES WITH A SUBTLE HINT OF FRUIT MAKES THIS 100% PURE UNSWEETENED CHOCOLATE SPECIAL.

65%

BALANCED AND SOPHISTICATED FLAVOURS
OF FRESH FRUITS WITH THE RIGHT LEVEL OF
SWEETNESS. DELICATE FLORAL NOTES ADD A
PERFECT FINALE.

72%

AN INTRIGUING PROVENANCE WITH DEEP
FRUIT NOTES WITH HINTS OF FRUITS. A RICH
AND INTERESTING TASTE WITH A PLEASING
FRUITINESS TO THE FINISH.

ROASTED NIBS

THIS IS THE PURE HEART OF THE CACAO BEAN. IT'S
THE ADDICTIVE, CRUNCHY, WHOLESOME GOODNESS
OF CACAO IN ITS PUREST FORM.

UNSWEETENED BAKING

STRONG, ROBUST AND INTENSE COCOA AROMAS
WITH EXCITING FLAVOURS OF FRUIT IN THIS
100% PURE CACAO.

MAMUSCHKA

— ARGENTINA —

Mamuschka is an exclusive chocolate producer situated in Bariloche, in Patagonia, Argentina, a region known for its chocolate. The business was founded over 29 years ago, and now includes retail outlets in Buenos Aires, San Martín and Villa la Angostura. Its philosophy is to create the most exquisite chocolate with the finest ingredients, and it has won numerous international awards in the process. Its premium chocolate range boasts several robust single-origin bars, with an impressive overall depth, richness and silky texture. All of its chocolates are bean-to-bar. The company also has designed immaculate packaging to further enhance its quality products.

For something extraordinary, choose the Barritas Oregon, a delicate yet intense chocolate bar.

BARRITAS OREGON

THIS BAR IS AN INTENSE DARK CHOCOLATE THAT HAS DELICATE
UNDERTONES OF FRAGRANT DRIED FRUITS.

70% CACAO & ALMENDRAS

THE CRUNCHY TEXTURE OF THE ALMONDS IS COMBINED WITH CRIOLLO CACAO,
GIVING THE CHOCOLATE A CITRIC TASTE AND EARTHY CHOCOLATE FLAVOUR.

76% CACAO AMARGO

THE ECUADORIAN CACAO USED IN THIS BAR HAS HINTS OF ORGANIC HONEY FROM THE FLOWERS OF THE ARGENTINE PAMPAS.

70% CACAO & FRUTOS

THIS CHOCOLATE HAS FLAVOURS OF ROASTED DRIED FRUITS AND PISTACHIOS, WITH A HINT OF CITRUS AND FLOWERS.

100% PERU

THE 100% BAR USES THE FINEST PERUVIAN CACAO, WHICH DISPLAYS NOTES OF GRAN BLANCO, CITRUS, MARACUYA, FLOWERS AND ORANGE.

BARRITAS ALERCE

THIS BAR, STUDDED WITH NUTS AND GOJI BERRIES, IS CRAFTED FROM PERUVIAN AND ECUADORIAN CACAO, WHICH GIVES A VIBRANT EARTHY TEXTURE, WITH DELICATE HINTS OF DRY FRUITS AND WHITE CANE SUGAR.

MARSATTA CHOCOLATE

~ USA ~

Marsatta is a specialist bean-to-bar chocolate factory located in Torrance, California, United States. The company was founded in 2003 by Canadian-born Jeffray D. Gardner (formerly a professional hockey referee) and his wife, Naomi. The business has grown over the years and it now includes a café. The fresh beans come from a farmer (and now family friend) in Belize, who hand-delivers these on a monthly basis. Jeffray carefully hand-crafts the single-origin bars from the sustainably produced beans to represent the natural flavours of their origin.

Don't miss the smooth 82% Super Raybar (containing 33 different organic super foods), which is a tribute to Jeffray's late father.

SUPER RAYBAR

ULTRA SMOOTH AND GENTLY FRUITY ORGANIC COCOA, PRESENTED WITH 33 DIFFERENT ORGANIC SUPER FOODS. THIS BAR HAS AN EXCELLENT CITRUS FINISH.

BON BONS

AROMATIC FRUITY HEIRLOOM ORGANIC COCOA COMBINED WITH THE FINEST
SEASONAL INGREDIENTS RESULTS IN A RICH ASSORTMENT OF BON BONS, WITH
AN EXTRAVAGANT MELT-IN-THE-MOUTH EXPERIENCE.

63

THIS FRUITY ORGANIC CHOCOLATE, PRESENTED AT A LOWER PERCENTAGE TO HIGHLIGHT ITS FRUIT FLAVOURS, HAS NOTES OF BLACKBERRY AND CANDIED PINEAPPLE.

74

THIS ULTRA SMOOTH, HEIRLOOM ORGANIC CHOCOLATE HAS A CREAMY TEXTURE, WITH NOTES OF BLACKBERRY, DRIED FIG AND CHERRY.

89

USING ORGANIC COCOA WITH A HIGHER CACAO PERCENTAGE, THIS IS THE CHOCOLATE FOR THOSE WHO CRAVE CACAO. IT HAS NOTES OF BLACKBERRY, CINNAMON AND A TANGY CITRUS FINISH.

100

MADE FROM HEIRLOOM CACAO, THIS IS A BAR WITH A DEEP, BOLD CHOCOLATE FINISH, AND NOTES OF BLACKBERRY, BLUEBERRY AND CANDIED PINEAPPLE.

MASHPI CHOCOLATE ARTESANAL

— ECUADOR —

Mashpi Chocolate Artesanal is a farm-based operation in Pichincha, Ecuador. It does not rely on modern technology and is free of chemical ingredients. Indeed, owners Agustina and Alejandro have committed their lives to rebuilding their land, restoring its biodiversity and protecting it from industrial farming. The company uses the highest grade of Ecuadorian Arriba Nacional cacao beans to create a completely organic product, subject to rigorous quality controls. All of the single-origin chocolate is processed using specialist traditional machinery to ensure the maximum flavour, while experimenting with biodiversity in different flavour profiles.

The creamy and fruity texture of its sublime Cacao Pulp bar is almost overwhelming.

CACAO PULP

THIS INNOVATIVE CREATION PROVIDES A UNIQUE EXPERIENCE WITH A SEMI-LIQUID CACAO FILLING, FULL OF FRUITY FLAVOURS, REFRESHING FLORAL AROMAS AND SOFT CARAMEL TONES.

GUAYABILLA

GUAYABILLA, A FRUIT EXCLUSIVE TO THE CHOCO RAINFOREST, ADDS THE PERFECT TOUCH OF ACIDITY, AND SUBTLE NOTES OF EUCALYPTUS TO THIS UNIQUE CHOCOLATE BAR

maShPi

chocolate artesanal

barra de chocolate con guayabilla

65% cacao

USDA ORGANIC

EC-BIO-144
Producto de Ecuador

65%

FALL BACK IN TIME TO ECUADOR'S
ANCESTRAL CACAO ROOTS. WITH
VIBRANT RED BERRY AND CITRUS
UNDERTONES, THIS IS
AN EXPERTLY BALANCED
CHOCOLATE BAR.

80%

AN ELIXIR FROM SINGLE-ORIGIN
MASHPI CACAO FOR TRUE LOVERS
OF THE DARK SIDE OF CHOCOLATE.
EXQUISITE EARTHY BEGINNINGS
EXPAND INTO COMPLEX TONES
OF NUTS, WOODS, AND SPICES.

70% NIBS

TOASTED CACAO BEANS
HIGHLIGHT THE RICH FLAVOURS OF
THE ARRIBA NACIONAL CACAO,
ADDING A BOOST TO ITS NATURAL
ANTIOXIDANTS.

CALAMONDIN

CALAMONDIN IS A SMALL
CITRUS FRUIT WITH A DELICATE,
AROMATIC SKIN THAT IS
CULTIVATED ALONGSIDE MASHPI
CACAO. THE CALAMONDIN'S
PEEL INFUSES THIS PERFECTLY
BALANCED CHOCOLATE BAR WITH
CITRIC TONES.

MASON & CO
— INDIA —

Mason & Co is situated in Tamil Nadu, India, and employs an all-female workforce, drawn from local villages. Jointly founded by Fabien (a former sound engineer) and Jane (a specialist raw chef/chocolatier), the company operates fair trade agreements with several farmers and ethically sources all of its cacao beans locally from Tamil Nadu and Kerala. All of its vegan gourmet products are organic, and free from chemicals, preservatives and emulsifiers, thereby preserving the flavour and health benefits of the cacao beans. The brand offers several robust single-origin bars, and intriguing flavour combinations, such as chilli and cinnamon, but all with luxurious taste profiles.

The standout is the alluring Rosemary & Sea Salt, with its unusual savoury combination that highlights the richness of the chocolate.

70%

ROSEMARY &
SEA SALT
DARK CHOCOLATE

MASON & CO
CRAFTSMEN OF CHOCOLATE

SINGLE ORIGIN
CACAO BEANS FROM INDIA
ORGANIC • VEGAN

MADE IN AUROVILLE

70 g

ROSEMARY & SEA SALT

AN UNUSUAL PAIRING SEES SEA SALT
COMBINED WITH THE DEEP AND ENTICING
FLAVOUR OF THE ROSEMARY. THE EFFECT
SERVES TO HIGHLIGHT THE SWEET RICH
CHOCOLATE NOTES OF THE
DARK CHOCOLATE.

70%

CHILLI & CINNAMON DARK CHOCOLATE

MASON & CO
CRAFTSMEN OF CHOCOLATE

SINGLE ORIGIN
CACAO BEANS FROM INDIA
ORGANIC+VEGAN

MADE IN AUROVILLE
70 g

CHILLI & CINNAMON

THIS BAR EXHIBITS
THE PERFECT BALANCE
OF SOFT CINNAMON
AND FIERY RED CHILLI
FLAKES, COMBINED WITH
SLIGHTLY SWEET RICH
DARK CHOCOLATE.

ZESTY ORANGE

BITTERSWEET DARK
CHOCOLATE IS COMBINED
WITH BITTER ZESTY ORAN
TO CREATE A FRESH AND
FRUITY BAR.

55%

COCONUT MILK DARK CHOCOLATE

MASON & CO
CRAFTSMEN OF CHOCOLATE

SINGLE ORIGIN

COCONUT MILK

A MILD 55% DARK CHOCOLATE BAR MIXED
WITH THE VEGAN GOODNESS OF SUBTLE
COCONUT MILK GIVES IT A SMOOTH
CREAMY MILK DARK CHOCOLATE FEEL

75%

ZESTY ORANGE
DARK CHOCOLATE

MASON & CO
CRAFTSMEN OF CHOCOLATE

SINGLE ORIGIN
CACAO BEANS FROM INDIA
ORGANIC+VEGAN

MADE IN AUROVILLE
70 g

75%

PEPPERMINT &
SWEET NIBS
DARK CHOCOLATE

MASON & CO
CRAFTSMEN OF CHOCOLATE

SINGLE ORIGIN
CACAO BEANS FROM INDIA
ORGANIC+VEGAN

MADE IN AUROVILLE
70 g

PEPPERMINT & SWEET NIBS

THE ULTIMATE COMBINATION OF COOLING MINT,
CRUNCHY SWEET CACAO NIBS AND SIGNATURE
75% CHOCOLATE, GIVING THE BAR TEXTURAL
INTEREST AND REFRESHING TONES.

65%

ESPRESSO
DARK CHOCOLATE

MASON & CO
CRAFTSMEN OF CHOCOLATE

SINGLE
CACAO

ESPRESSO

THIS IS A BOLD-TASTING BAR.
THE PERFECT BALANCE OF
ORGANIC SINGLE-ESTATE COFFEE
AND SEMI-SWEET CHOCOLATE.
IT HAS A SLIGHT BITTERNESS
AND BEAUTIFUL FRUITY NOTES.

MONSIEUR TRUFFE

— AUSTRALIA —

Monsieur Truffe is an award-winning Melbourne-based chocolate maker in Australia specialising in high-quality organic products and memorable chocolate products. Starting as a one-man operation in 2006, Monsieur Truffe originally sold its wickedly delicious products at a local market but has since expanded. All of its natural, preservative and gluten-free chocolate is made from the finest cacao, which is ethically sourced from farmers worldwide. Samanta, the chocolatier, takes great care with the beans when roasting or conching, seeking to showcase the optimal tasting notes. The brand uses packaging made from recycled paper. All of its dark chocolate is vegan.

The Salt-Roasted Pistachios bar has a fabulous crunchy texture and slightly savoury taste.

SALT-ROASTED PISTACHIOS

VIBRANT, CRUNCHY AND SLIGHTLY SALTY, THIS CHOCOLATE BAR COMBINES
SINGLE-ORIGIN AND MILDLY ACIDIC DARK CHOCOLATE FROM THE DOMINICAN
REPUBLIC WITH SALT-ROASTED PISTACHIOS.

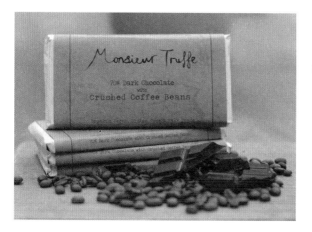

CRUSHED COFFEE BEANS

FULL-BODIED FRUITY FLAVOURED DARK CHOCOLATE IS TEAMED WITH CRUSHED ARABICA COFFEE BEANS.

CHAI

SMOOTH, FRAGRANT AND DELICIOUS AYURVEDIC CHAI BLEND IS COMBINED WITH WELL-BALANCED DARK CHOCOLATE TO CREATE THE MOST SOOTHING EXPERIENCE EVER.

HONEYCOMB

INSPIRED BY AN EDWARDIAN BRITISH CHOCOLATE CANDY BAR, THIS IS A PLAYFUL AND DELIGHTFUL MARRIAGE BETWEEN INTENSE CHOCOLATE AND LIP-SMACKING HONEYCOMB.

RUM & RAISIN

FRAGRANT SMOKED RUM MIXED WITH THE SWEETEST SULTANAS, RAISINS AND DARK CHOCOLATE BOND TOGETHER TO CREATE THIS HARMONIOUS SYMPHONY OF FLAVOURS.

ECUADOR

FULL-BODIED RICH CHOCOLATE WITH A VELVETY MELT AND A LUSCIOUS CREAMY MOUTH-FEEL WITH CARAMEL AND CITRUS NOTES.

NAHUA CHOCOLATE

— COSTA RICA —

Nahua Chocolate is probably the most exclusive craft chocolate producer in Costa Rica. The company is dedicated to improving the lives of local farmers by operating a Cacao Renovation Program. This initiative provides invaluable technical training, financial assistance and promotes sustainable farming practices. As well as contributing to the environment the company also makes exquisite chocolate. All of its premium single-origin bars contain Trinitario cacao beans combined with the finest quality organic ingredients. To complete the picture, the bars are wrapped in colourful bespoke packaging inspired by the Costa Rican jungle.

Enjoy the potent full-bodied flavour of the Coffee bar, best consumed slowly with a fine glass of red wine.

ALMONDS

EXQUISITE HEIRLOOM CACAO IS PAIRED
WITH LIGHTLY ROASTED ALMONDS TO
DELIVER A BOLD TASTE SATISFACTION.

CHAI LATTE

FINE COSTA RICAN CHOCOLATE INFUSED
WITH A WARM BLEND OF TROPICAL SPICES
AND DELICATE BLACK TEA NOURISHES THE
BODY AND SOUL.

LEMONGRASS

THE DELICATE CITRUS ESSENCE OF
LEMONGRASS COMPLEMENTS THE FRUITY
CACAO, AND PROVIDES A REFRESHING AND
ENERGISING EXPERIENCE

NIBS

CRUNCHY ROASTED NIBS SURROUNDED IN
VELVETY FINE DARK CHOCOLATE PROVIDES
A FULL FLAVONOID EXPLOSION.

AT NAHUA WE HAVE A UNIQUE RELATIONSHIP WITH THE FARMERS THAT GROW OUR CACAO AND THE
CHOCOLATE WE CREATE. OUR TREE-TO-BAR MODEL ALLOWS US TO EXPERIMENT WITH DIFFERENT FERMEN-
TATION CYCLES AND SHARE SAMPLES OF NEW FLAVOURS AND DISTINCTIVE AROMAS WITH FARMERS.

WE ARE COMMITTED TO HELPING REVITALISE THE FINE CACAO MARKET IN COSTA RICA AND
REMAIN DEDICATED TO PRODUCING GOURMET PRODUCTS WITH AWARD-WINNING CACAO SOURCED
DIRECTLY FROM SMALLHOLDER FARMING FAMILIES.

Juan Pablo Büchert, FOUNDER, NAHUA CHOCOLATE

ORANGE

THIS CLASSIC TWIST OF CITRUS COMBINED
WITH PREMIUM CACAO DELIVERS
A HARMONIOUS BALANCE OF DEEP
TROPICAL NOTES.

OCHO
— NEW ZEALAND —

OCHO (short for 'Otago Chocolate') is a thriving business located in the popular city of Dunedin, New Zealand. The brand is the brainchild of former artist and journalist Liz Rowe, and its premises are in a trendy warehouse precinct. After a visit to Mexico in 2011 she became passionate about chocolate making and had a radical change of career. Clearly she has a knack for it because the taste is exceptionally rich, well balanced and completely moreish. OCHO sources all the cacao beans from farmers in the Pacific Islands, and seeks to showcase the different flavours. OCHO won gold in the 2018 New Zealand Chocolate Awards.

The hands-down winner is the Beekeeper, with raw honey and pollen, which heightens the flavours of the chocolate.

BEEKEEPER

MANUKA HONEY AND BEE POLLEN
DEEPEN THE BERRY FLAVOURS OF
THE 70% CHOCOLATE, WHILE PUFFED
AMARANTH GIVES A SOFT CRUNCH
REMINISCENT OF HONEY ON TOAST.

MY FAVOURITE BARS ARE THE PLAIN ONES THAT SHOWCASE THE DIFFERENCES BETWEEN CACAO BEANS FROM VARIOUS COUNTRIES AND AREAS – WE CALL THESE DARK CRAFT BARS. CHOCOLATE MAKES A GREAT SNACK AT ANY TIME OF THE DAY, BUT FOR ME A LITTLE SOMETHING WITH MORNING COFFEE AND AS AN AFTER-DINNER TREAT ARE THE PERFECT TIMES TO ENJOY. I EAT DIFFERENT FLAVOURS DEPENDING ON MY MOOD AND I WOULD ENCOURAGE EVERY CHOCOLATE LOVER TO EXPLORE THE WEALTH OF ORIGINS AND STYLES TO BE FOUND IN THE WORLD OF CRAFT CHOCOLATE.

Liz Rowe, FOUNDER, OCHO

SOLOMONS 70%.
THIS BAR IS FRUIT DRIVEN, WITH LIGHT CITRUS NOTES AND A RASPBERRY FINISH.

SOLOMONS 100%

A STRONG CHOCOLATE AROMA COMBINES WITH A
SURPRISINGLY CREAMY MOUTH FEEL, BRINGING
SOFT UMAMI NOTES AND A HINT OF GRAPEFRUIT.

PNG 88%

THINK TOBACCO AND UMAMI FLAVOURS WITH AN
UNDERLYING HINT OF BERRIES AND WHITE PEPPER
WITH THIS BAR.

HOROPITO & KAWAKAWA

TWO NEW ZEALAND NATIVE PLANTS GIVE SPICED
GINGER, CARDAMOM AND ALLSPICE FLAVOUR
NOTES, WITH A GENTLE PEPPERY FINISH.

SHORT BLACK

COFFEE AND VANILLA ADD DEPTH OF FLAVOUR TO
THE 70% CHOCOLATE, THEN ROASTED COCOA NIBS
ADD CRUNCH FOR A HIT OF ENERGY.

ORIGIN CHOCOLATE

— AUSTRALIA —

Origin is a craft chocolate producer located in New South Wales, Australia. The company is owned and operated by Matt Chimenti who is passionate about health and well-being, and writes a blog promoting the medical benefits of raw cacao. Origin only uses fair trade (or rainforest alliance), certified organic cacao in its products, which are additionally high in antioxidants. These beans are ethically sourced from a total of eight different countries, and each bar is named after its country of origin. Each chocolate has a solid identity, with an overall broad diversity in the range of complex flavours. Until recently the brand only produced single-origin bars but now it has introduced some new and tantalising flavours.

The rich and indulgent Peru 85% bar with its impressive taste notes will become your new favourite treat.

PERU

MADE FROM PERUVIAN CRIOLLO CACAO, THIS IS A FLAVOUR
POWERHOUSE WITH MASSIVE HITS OF RASPBERRY BEFORE ENDING ON
SOME CITRUS NOTES, WITH A LONG FINISH.

BRAZIL 69%

ORIGIN®
organic chocolate makers

Australian
Certified
Organic

NET WEIGHT 100gm

BRAZIL

THIS CHOCOLATE HAS A
DENSE CREAMY MOUTH
FEEL, AND CONTAINS
NOTES OF TOASTED
MACADAMIA NUTS, WOOD,
AS WELL AS TOFFEE, RED
FRUITS, VANILLA
AND TOBACCO.

DOMINICAN REPUBLIC

THIS CHOCOLATE HAS AN UNDERSTATED COMPLEXITY, WITH NOTES OF WOOD, SPICES, AND A PALATE OF PLUM, RUM AND RAISINS.

ECUADOR

MADE USING TRINATARIO BEANS, THIS IS A FULL-FLAVOURED CHOCOLATE WITH HITS OF CREAMY MACADAMIA NUTS, TOFFEE, VANILLA AND BURNT BUTTER.

GHANA

CONTAINS AROMAS OF VANILLA AND PEACH, WITH HINTS OF TOBACCO AND RAISIN, AND A CLASSIC EARTHY CHOCOLATE NOTE BEFORE FINISHING ON A NOTE OF BITTER COFFEE.

UGANDA

A RICHLY FLAVOURED CHOCOLATE WITH INTENSE AROMAS, AND NOTES WHICH INCLUDE CARAMEL, NUTS AND APRICOT.

POD CHOCOLATE
— INDONESIA —

Started by Australian-born chocoholic Toby Garritt, Pod Chocolate, Bali, is recognised as one of the finest chocolate companies in Southeast Asia. It all began with curiosity: Toby wanted to know how the cacao is transformed into chocolate, and why chocolate wasn't made where it was grown. From there, he set out to establish an ethical and sustainable business that supports local communities. Its products, with their broad spectrum of sophisticated flavour notes, are soon to be exported to selected countries. Recently Toby has been experimenting with organic Lontar palm flower nectar as a healthy alternative to sugar, which opens up a new taste dimension.

The elegant Sea Salt & Cacao Nibs bar is a must.

CRUNCHY CACAO NIBS SPARK WITH
BALINESE SEA SALT CRYSTALS,
WHICH ELEVATE THE ORGANIC
NECTAR WHILE BALANCING
PERFECTLY WITH THE LOCALLY
GROWN CACAO.

pod

Sea Salt & Cacao Nibs

64% dark chocolate sweetened with organic nectar

100g / 3.5oz

BANANA CHIPS & CLOVE

SWEETENED WITH ORGANIC LONTAR PALM
FLOWER NECTAR, THIS BAR IS A TRIBUTE
TO THE SPICE TRADE THAT PUT INDONESIA
ON THE MAP, AND IS CRUNCHY,
RICH AND EXOTIC.

MY FARMERS LOOK UP AND SEE A PLANE LEAVING BALI AIRPORT, HEADING TO EUROPE,
NORTH AMERICA OR AUSTRALIA, AND THEY KNOW THERE IS GOING TO BE POD
CHOCOLATE IN SOMEBODY'S HAND LUGGAGE. THAT MAKES THEM PROUD.

Toby Garritt, FOUNDER, POD CHOCOLATE

BALI 64%

THIS IS A CLASSIC-STYLE COUVERTURE
DARK CHOCOLATE BAR WITH SWEET
RAISIN NOTES AND NUTTY OVERTONES.

GOJI BERRY & COCONUT

A HEALTHY AND DELICIOUS BAR PACKED
WITH ANTIOXIDANTS AND SWEETENED
WITH UNREFINED NECTAR. THE CHEWY
GOJI BERRIES BEAUTIFULLY COMPLEMENT
THE CRUMBLE OF TOASTED COCONUT.

PRIVATE STASH

PREMIUM DARK CHOCOLATE MADE FROM
THE FINEST BEANS CREATES A SMOOTH
AND BUTTERY TEXTURE WITH A DEEP
RICHNESS AND LINGERING MOUTH FEEL
THAT IS SIMPLY EXQUISITE.

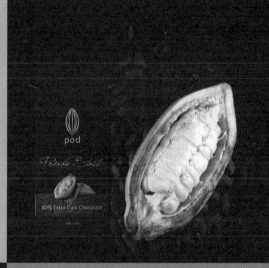

ROSELLA FLOWER & CASHEW

ROSELLA FLOWERS LEND TART, CITRUS
NOTES TO THE CRUMBLING CASHEW NUTS,
LINGERING NICELY AGAINST A BACKDROP
OF NUTTY DARK CHOCOLATE SWEETENED
WITH ORGANIC NECTAR.

RANGER CHOCOLATE COMPANY

— USA —

Ranger is a small artisanal chocolate company based in Portland, Oregon. All of its delicious bars are tempered, moulded and handwrapped (in distinctive packaging) at its own production facility. Ranger uses cacao beans largely from Peru but also from Haiti, Vietnam, Colombia, Guatemala and Belize. The folks at Ranger also believe in pairing chocolate with coffee, wine and foods, making the robust taste and texture a perfect match with other gourmet foods. As well as a variety of single-origin bars, it also offers candied nibs and chocolate caramel sauce.

Usually 100% cacao bars can be overbearing but the intensity of Ranger's 100% Peru bar works beautifully, producing an overall accessible extreme dark bar.

_ᗋ · ᗋ · ᗋ · ᗋ · ᗋ_

100% PERU

AT 100% CACAO, THIS BAR IS
INTENSE, YET APPROACHABLE.
IT HAS NOTES OF RAW
ALMOND, TAMARIND AND A
HINT OF SESAME; AND IT'S
SUGAR-FREE.

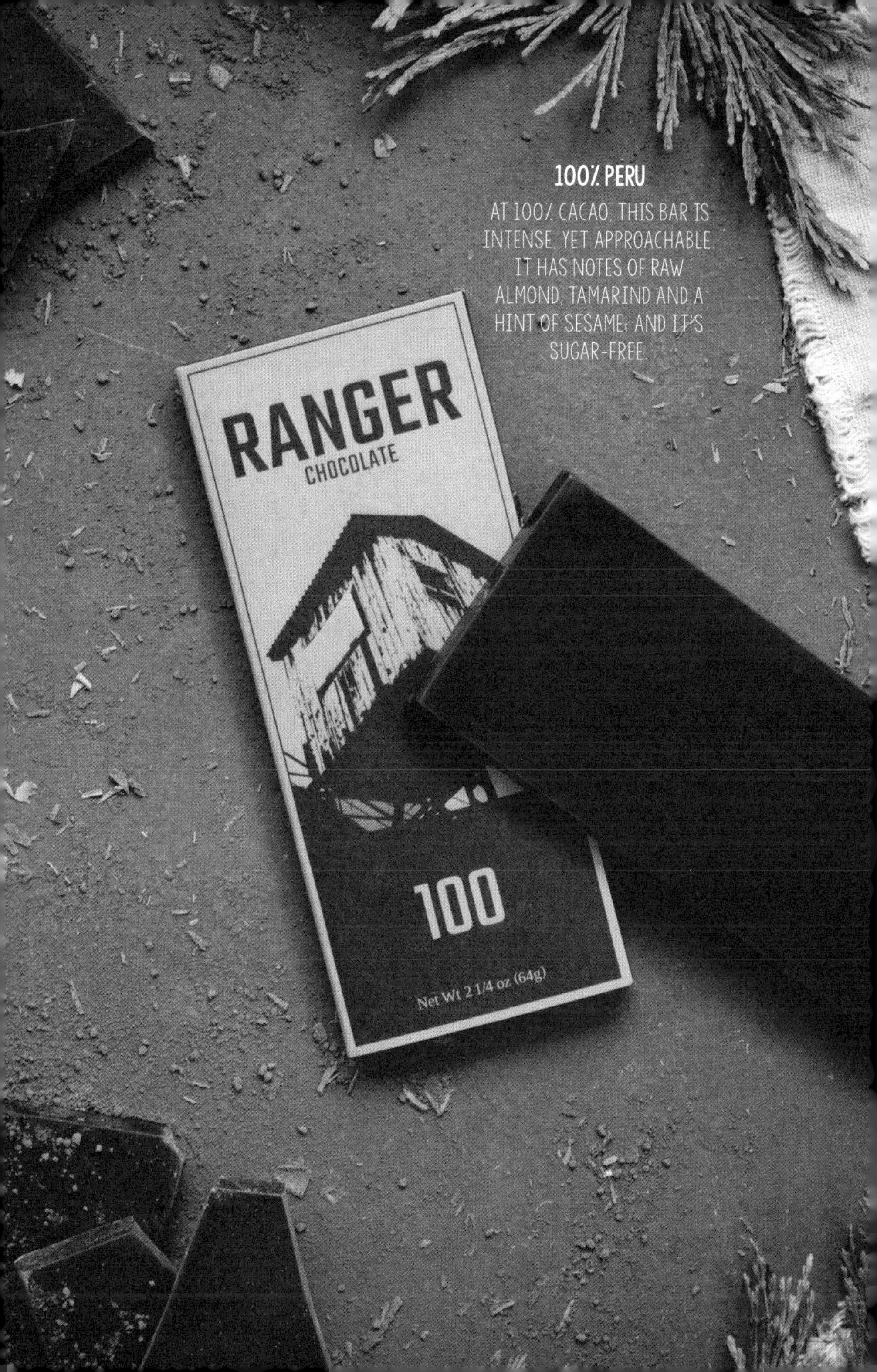

RANGER
CHOCOLATE

100

Net Wt 2 1/4 oz (64g)

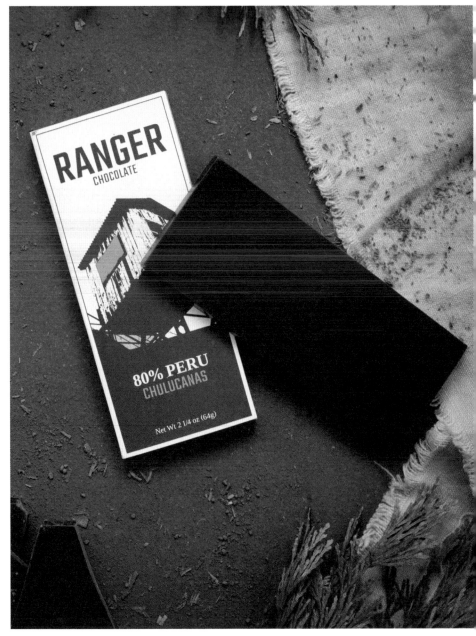

80% PERU CHULUCANAS

DELICATE AND SWEET, ITS EARTHY TONES – WITH NOTES OF BLACK WALNUT AND DARK
BERRIES – CAN BE ENJOYED WITH A GLASS OF RED WINE OR BARREL-AGED WHISKEY.

72% PERU SALITRAL

FRUIT FORWARD WITH NOTES OF STONE
FRUIT AND HONEYSUCKLE, IT ENDS ON A BOLD
STRAWBERRY FINISH. TRY PAIRING IT WITH YOUR
FAVOURITE IPA.

70% PERU PIURA

CACAO FORWARD WITH NOTES OF TRUFFLE AND A
BLACK CHERRY FINISH, THIS IS WELL BALANCED
WITH A CREAMY SMOOTH TEXTURE. IT'S THE
PERFECT COMPANION FOR A GLASS OF RED WINE.

70% PERU SAN MARTÌN

THIS IS VERY BOLD WITH TANNINS AND A DRY
FINISH. EXPECT EARTHY TASTING NOTES, WITH A
HINT OF STRAWBERRY AND APRICOT. TRY IT WITH
A HEARTY RED WINE OR AN IPA.

WILDCARD

THE WILDCARD IS AN EXPERIMENTAL BAR
MADE USING DIFFERENT BEANS AND ROASTING
TECHNIQUES, AND EACH BATCH IS DIFFERENT.
YOU'LL HAVE TO GUESS THE NOTES ON THIS ONE!

RAWR

— UK —

RAWR is a specialist independent food producer located in the idyllic region of East Anglia, United Kingdom. The award-winning company originally started life in a home kitchen and has significantly grown. All of its chocolate is made at low temperatures to preserve the enzymes and other beneficial compounds, and retaining the cacao's deep and complex taste. Its completely natural, vegan, gluten- and dairy-free raw chocolate bars are now sold in exclusive retailers in the UK and Europe. The texture might be different to conventional chocolate, but the intense flavour doesn't disappoint. The eye-catching packaging made with recycled materials (including cocoa shell) gives the bars a vibrant and unique appearance.

Sample the Lucuma Cacao bar for its smoothness and sumptuous flavour.

LUCUMA CACAO

VELVETY SMOOTH, WITH A
SUMPTUOUS, TANGY, CARAMEL-
LIKE FLAVOUR FROM THE
PERUVIAN LUCUMA FRUIT AND
COCONUT PALM SUGAR.

GOJI BERRIES & VANILLA

WHOLE, ANTIOXIDANT-RICH GOJI
BERRIES LEND A SWEET TANG TO THE
CHOCOLATE, AND ARE COMPLEMENTED
BY MADAGASCAN VANILLA.

MINT

LUXURIOUSLY CHOCOLATEY WITH THE VIGOUR OF MINT, NATURE'S ORIGINAL APERITIF, THIS BAR REFRESHES AND SATISFIES.

ORANGE

A DEEP SWELL OF CHOCOLATE BRUSHED WITH ORGANIC ORANGE OIL RESULTS IN A LIGHT, TANGY, AND UTTERLY DECADENT TASTE EXPERIENCE.

68%

RICH CHOCOLATE INFUSED WITH MADAGASCAN VANILLA, GIVEN DEPTH AND A FRUITY COMPLEXITY BY CAROB AND LUCUMA.

80%

80% CACAO, LOW IN SUGAR, WITH JUST A HINT OF VANILLA AND LUCUMA FRUIT PROVIDES A HIGH CACAO CONTENT HIT FOR EXTREME CHOCOLATE LOVERS.

SEATONFIRE CHILLI CHOCOLATE

— AUSTRALIA —

Seatonfire is a natural food producer located in southeastern Queensland, Australia, and is run from the family farm by mother and son team Lynne Seaton-Anderson and Jason O'Connor. The company grows its own chemical-free organic chilli and incorporates it into its premium range of chocolate bars, developing a range of exciting flavour combinations to tantalise your tastebuds. The sensational taste and heat intensity vary from bar to bar. While some of the varieties are admittedly spicy, these are not too overbearing and the hints of chilli do not detract from the refined cacao taste.

The mellow flavours of the Salted Caramel bar make a great starting point.

SALTED CARAMEL

AN INTOXICATING SCENT OF SWEET, LUSCIOUS CARAMEL,
SILKY SMOOTH DARK CHOCOLATE AND SCATTERED SEA SALT
WITH SUBTLE CHILLI. PAIR WITH CHAMPAGNE.

LIQUORICE & LIME

ZINGY AND FRESH FLAVOUR NOTES FROM FARM-GROWN LIME ZEST,
WITH TOASTED ANISEED CRUNCH AND SMOOTH LIQUORICE FLAVOUR,
WRAPPED IN DARK CHOCOLATE. PAIR WITH TEMPRANILLO.

MILD CHAI

HOUSE-GROUND CHAI SPICES INFUSED WITH MILD ORGANIC CHILLI TO PRODUCE A SILKY SMOOTH CHOCOLATE WITH A SUBTLE WARMTH. PAIR WITH A CHAI TEA OR WHISKEY.

WILD ORANGE

THE FLAVOUR JOURNEY BEGINS WITH PIQUANT ORANGE, DARK CHOCOLATE AND THEN WARM ORGANIC CHILLI TO PLEASURE THE PALATE. PAIR WITH A FLORAL SEMILLON.

WILD ROSEMARY & SEA SALT

ROSEMARY IN DARK CHOCOLATE AND SPRINKLED WITH SEA SALT IS A TASTE SENSATION. WITH HINTS OF ROAST LAMB AND CHOCOLATE PUDDING. PAIR WITH SPARKLING SHIRAZ.

WILD SESAME

TOASTED SESAME SEEDS IN DARK CHOCOLATE ADD A TEXTURAL ELEMENT AND LINGERING NUTTY NOTES. FOLLOWED WITH A FIERY CHILLI PUNCH. SERVE WITH COLD IPA.

SHE UNIVERSE

— NEW ZEALAND —

She Universe is an exclusive chocolate producer situated in the iconic location of Christchurch, New Zealand, and co-owned by passionate chocolatier Oonagh Browne. As well as practising traditional European-style (couverture) techniques, the company also handcrafts directly from Samoan and Peruvian cacao beans. This means that customers can experience a huge variety of taste profiles. Oonagh also runs workshops for discerning consumers with an appetite for knowledge and fine chocolate. The range includes some intriguingly named products and flavour combinations.

For an engaging and spicy taste experience, try the extraordinary Chilli & Cacao Nibs bar.

MANDARIN & ORANGE

THE NOTES OF ORANGE START TO ACTIVATE THE MIDDLE OF THE TASTING PALATE AND AWAKEN DEEPER NOTES OF MARMALADE AND HONEY, FINISHING WITH A CLEAR ZINGING ORANGE NOTE.

PINEAPPLE & BASIL

PINEAPPLE BRINGS A NEW TEXTURE AND TASTE AS THE BASIL AND PINEAPPLE MERGE INTO THE CREAMY CHOCOLATE, WITH HINTS OF BALSAMIC AND LIQUORICE.

RASPBERRY

STRONG RASPBERRY NOTES PEAK INSTANTLY THEN DROP DEEPLY INTO THE CACAO BEFORE MERGING INTO A FRUITS OF THE FOREST EXPERIENCE, WITH BLUEBERRIES TO WILD BOYSENBERRIES.

SEA SALT

THE INCLUSION OF THE SALT ENHANCES AND ENRICHES THE CARAMEL, LIQUORICE, FRUIT AND LAVENDER NOTES THAT ARE DELICATE IN THE CHOCOLATE, HIGHLIGHTING THE FLAVOURS AND SUBTLETIES.

PASSION FRUIT, GINGER & LEMON

PASSION FRUIT AND GINGER BURST FORTH ON THE PALATE BEFORE SETTLING DOWN IN THE CHOCOLATE NOTES.

SOLSTICE CHOCOLATE

— USA —

Solstice is an award-winning bean-to-bar artisan chocolate maker situated in Salt Lake City, Utah. The business is operated by creative powerhouse DeAnn Wallin who is passionate about good wholesome food. Solstice uses the finest quality ingredients and sources all of its cacao beans from farmers around the world on a fair trade basis. The range includes several single-origin varieties, each with the country of origin clearly indicated. The chocolate has a full-rounded, smooth and satisfying taste, a quality best appreciated in its magnificent Wasatch bar. As an eco-friendly touch, the bright packaging is recyclable and also resealable for ease of use.

The Wasatch bar, with its warm cinnamon notes, is an unforgettable taste sensation.

WASATCH

PLEASANT CINNAMON AND COMFORTING COCOA NOTES MINGLE
IN THIS ORIGINAL BLEND. THE NAME COMES FROM THE WASATCH
MOUNTAINS IN UTAH, WHERE SOLSTICE IS BASED.

BOLIVIA PALOS BLANCOS

THE BEANS ARE SOURCED FROM A DAMP, RAINY REGION OF BOLIVIA, GIVING THE CHOCOLATE DELICATE FRUIT NOTES THAT TRANSFORM TO A SWIRL OF MILD CREAM, NUTS AND HONEY.

THE SHINE AND SNAP OF CHOCOLATE THAT'S BEEN WELL CRAFTED AND TEMPERED IS A BEAUTIFUL WORK OF ART TO BE SAVOURED. I LOVE WHEN PEOPLE TELL ME THEIR CHOCOLATE STORIES. GIVING IT AS A GIFT, SHARING IT WITH FRIENDS, KEEPING A HIDDEN STASH OF BARS FOR THEMSELVES, MAKING IT A PART OF A HOLIDAY OR SPECIAL OCCASION, OR SNACKING ON A BAR TO GET THEM THROUGH THEIR WORK DAY: THESE ARE SOME OF THE EXPERIENCES SHARED WITH ME.

DeAnn Wallin, OWNER/CHOCOLATE MAKER, SOLSTICE CHOCOLATE

ECUADOR CAMINO VERDE

DEEP WALNUT AND PECAN FLAVOURS ARE FOLLOWED BY CARAMEL AND BROWN SUGAR NOTES WITH A HINT OF BANANA.

MADAGASCAR SAMBIRANO

BOLD CITRUS NOTES TRUMPET THROUGH
THIS BRIGHT CHOCOLATE, ENLIVENING
THE SENSES WITH A TANGY PUNCH.

TANZANIA KILOMBERO

THE TASTE OF HONEYSUCKLE WEAVES
AROUND NOTES OF WINE, WITH THE ZEST
OF LEMON PUNCTUATED BY THE FLORAL
SWEETNESS.

UGANDA BUNDIBUGYO

A DARK-TASTING CHOCOLATE THAT IS
REMINISCENT OF THE PERFECT BROWNIE:
NUTTY, CHOCOLATEY AND BREADY, WITH
FRESH EARTHY HINTS OF BERRIES.

STONE GRINDZ CHOCOLATE

— USA —

Stone Grindz is a wholesome craft food producer located in Scottsdale, Arizona. The company is owned by dynamic duo Steven Shipler and Kasey McCaslin who like to be involved in every stage of the process. This means building sustainable alliances with farmers, and fermenting, roasting, grinding and moulding the cacao into delicious chocolate treats. Varieties include robust single-origin bars and mouth-watering flavours like Red Raspberry or Cinnamon Cayenne, to name but just a few. The bars might be small in size but they each pack a mean punch on the taste front. The custom-made packaging, reminiscent of a stained glass window, is just divine.

Don't go past the extravagant Almond & Sea Salt bar, with its successful union of sweet and savoury.

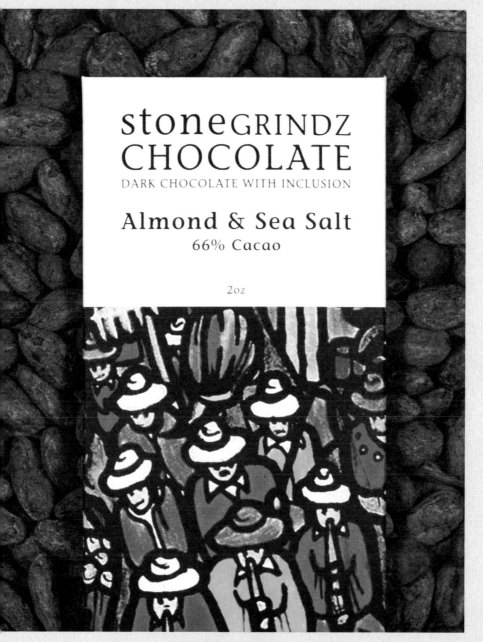

stoneGRINDZ CHOCOLATE

DARK CHOCOLATE WITH INCLUSION

Almond & Sea Salt
66% Cacao

2oz

ALMOND & SEA SALT

A MIXTURE OF DARK CHOCOLATE WITH CRUNCHY ROASTED
ALMONDS AND PLAYFUL TOUCHES OF PURE SEA SALT THAT
INTENSIFY THE NUTTY CARAMEL NOTES.

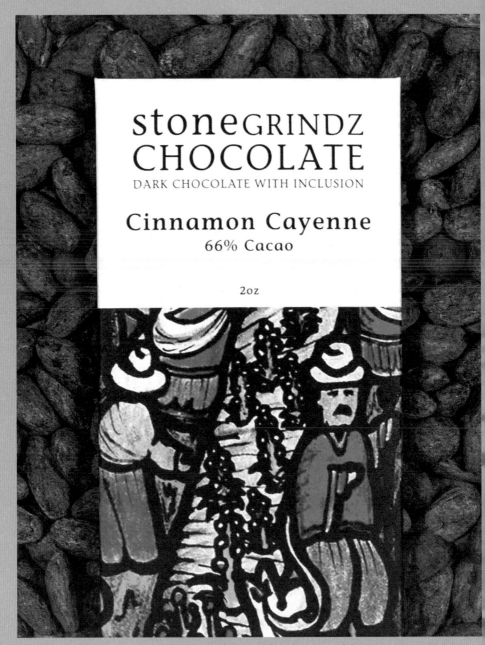

stoneGRINDZ
CHOCOLATE

DARK CHOCOLATE WITH INCLUSION

Cinnamon Cayenne
66% Cacao

2oz

CINNAMON CAYENNE

THIS IS A RICH DARK CHOCOLATE WITH NOTES OF RED FRUIT, CARAMEL
AND FUDGE BEFORE BUILDING TO LAYERS OF WARM CINNAMON
AND LINGERING CAYENNE PEPPER.

ESMERALDAS, ECUADOR

MADE FROM ECUADORIAN CACAO BEANS, THIS
CHOCOLATE HAS A BRIGHT CHARACTER WITH
NOTES OF FUDGE, PLUM AND RAISIN.

HACIENDA VICTORIA

LIGHTLY ROASTED ECUADORIAN BEANS PROVIDE
CLARITY OF FLAVOUR WITH NOTES OF ALMOND
BUTTER, TOAST AND RAISIN.

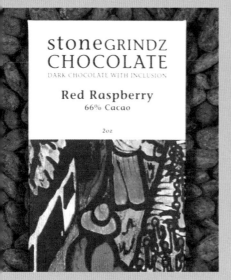

RED RASPBERRY

THIS BAR HAS AN EXPLOSION OF TART RASPBERRY
FLAVOUR, WITH TOFFEE NOTES FOLLOWED BY A
BALANCED FINISH.

WILD BOLIVIA

CRAFTED FROM WILD-GROWN CACAO BEANS,
THIS CHOCOLATE BAR CONTAINS NOTES OF
ROASTED MALT, CASHEW AND PLUM.

TABAL CHOCOLATE

— USA —

Tabal is the Mayan word for relationship, and it is the ability of chocolate to bring people together that fuels the passion of Tabal Chocolate. In 2017 Tabal opened its first retail store in Wauwatosa, Wisconsin, United States, having been established by Dan Bieser at his home only five years earlier. His primary objective as a chocolatier was to produce some of the finest bean-to-bar chocolate on the market. He has achieved this by using the finest cacao beans, which are roasted and stone ground by hand in small batches. The result is a range of tasty single-origin and flavoured bars. The overall success of the brand lies in the integrity and purity of the ingredients used.

The Perú + Cherries bar is an unforgettable melt-in-the-mouth experience.

tabal™

chocolate

great chocolate, greater relationships.

PERÚ

peruvian single source cacao

+ CHERRIES

USDA ORGANIC

K KOSHER PARVE

70% CACAO
FAIRLY TRADED
BEAN TO BAR

WT. 3 oz (85 g)

GROUND
ein

PERÚ + CHERRIES

TART DRIED ORGANIC CHERRIES ENHANCE THE NATURAL FRUITINESS OF THE PERUVIAN SINGLE-ORIGIN CACAO WITH ACCENTS OF CITRUS BLOOM AND POMEGRANATE

Kä

Two Ingredient Chocolate

NICARAGUA

 KOSHER PARVE

70% CACAO
BEAN TO BAR

DIRECT TRADE

tabal™
chocolate

NET WT 3 oz (85 g)

NICARAGUA

THIS CHOCOLATE MADE FROM JUST TWO
INGREDIENTS HAS A COMPLEX FLAVOUR PROFILE,
WITH NOTES OF CARAMEL, NUTS AND FRUIT.

COLOMBIA

CACAO FROM THE COLOMBIAN ANDES REVEALS A RICH, BOLD COCOA FLAVOUR WITH NOTES OF CARAMEL, BANANA AND A HINT OF CITRUS.

DOMINICAN ESPRESSO CRUNCH

MADE FROM SINGLE-ORIGIN DOMINICAN REPUBLIC CACAO. THE FLAVOUR NOTES INCLUDE COFFEE, CARAMEL AND SWEET DRIED FRUITS.

COSTA RICA + SEA SALT

FINE FLAKE SEA SALT HELPS GIVE A SAVOURY BALANCE BETWEEN SEMI-SWEET AND SALTY, WITH NOTES OF CITRUS AND CARAMEL.

MASALA CHAI

A HINT OF SPICE WITH AROMATIC GUATEMALAN CARDAMOM, HOT AND CITRUSY GINGER, SWEET CINNAMON, AND ACCENTS OF CRACKED BLACK PEPPER AND FRAGRANT CLOVES.

TONANTZIN CHOCOLATE

— AUSTRALIA —

Tonantzin, an artisan family-owned business, derives its distinctive name from the Aztec word for Sacred Mother Earth. Located in the verdant hills of the Yarra Valley, near Melbourne, Australia, the company was established by Fernando Ramirez and Antonia Green, and is dedicated to producing chocolate that embodies the sacred origins of cacao. All of its vegan bean-to-bar raw chocolate is made in micro batches to ensure optimum flavour and vitality from the Criollo cacao. The brand's choice of eclectic flavours, like Purple Corn & Açai, Maya Nut & Amaranth and Lime & Prickly Pear, ensures it stands out from the crowd. All these varieties are superb, providing an incredible taste sensation. Its bars are embossed with a decorative pattern that is a replica of Aztec stone carvings, and enveloped in distinctive eco-friendly packaging.

The Chilli, Mango & Mezquite bar is the highlight in the range with its smooth tones and warm chilli finish.

CHILLI MANGO MEZQUITE

JOURNEY THROUGH THE CARAMEL TONES OF PROTEIN-RICH MEZQUITE TO THE FRUITY PUNCH OF MANGO, ENDING IN A WARM TOUCH OF CHILLI.

TONANTZIN

AZTEC ARTISAN CHOCOLATE

CHILLI ◆ MANGO ◆ MEZQUITE

ORGANIC RAW DARK CHOCOLATE

◆ HANDMADE IN THE YARRA VALLEY ◆

65% CRIOLLO CACAO   55g NET

AZTEC EGG WITH CASHEW GANACHE

A DELUXE SOFT CENTRE OF CASHEW
BUTTER AND DARK CHOCOLATE, ENCASED
IN 60% CRIOLLO CACAO DARK CHOCOLATE
AND DUSTED WITH GOLD.

LIME & PRICKLY PEAR

WITH ITS UNIQUE TART FLAVOUR, PRICKLY PEAR LIES DEEP IN AZTEC MYTH. COUPLED WITH ZESTY LIME, THIS IS A VIBRANT COMBINATION.

MAYA NUT & AMARANTH

LIGHTLY TEXTURED WITH WARM COFFEE OVERTONES, THIS BLEND COMBINES TWO ANCIENT SUPER FOODS THAT NOURISH AND ENERGISE.

PURE DARK

THE DEEP POTENT FLAVOUR TONES OF HEIRLOOM CRIOLLO CACAO IN ITS PURITY, SWEETENED WITH

PURPLE CORN & AÇAI

WITH AMAZONIAN AÇAI BERRY, HIBISCUS AND THE EARTHY GOODNESS OF PURPLE CORN, THIS

VICUÑA CHOCOLATE

— USA —

Vicuña is a chocolate factory and retailer based in Peterborough, New Hampshire, United States. The company is the brainchild of Neely Cohen, but was bought in 2017 by Casey Goodrich and Nate Morison who want to continue Neely's good work. All the gourmet single-origin bars are made from just two simple ingredients (cacao and raw cane sugar). By sticking to this winning formula, the refined rich taste shines through, leaving the happy customer craving for more. The company name derives from the vicuña, a South American alpaca which dates back to Incan times, known for the rarity and quality of its fleece.

Each variety is delicious, but in particular the Dominican + Sea Salt bar is unmissable.

DOMINICAN + SALT

SALT SIDE DOWN ALLOWS
THE CURRANT NOTE OF THE
DOMINICAN CHOCOLATE TO
HANG BACK WHILE THE SALT
ENGAGES WITH THE PEANUT
AND RUM NOTES.

BELIZE

PLEASANTLY SMOOTH
CHOCOLATE ALLOWS NOTES
OF CREAMY BROWNED BUTTER
TO WASH OVER THE TONGUE,
FINISHING WITH A SUBTLE
NAVEL ORANGE NOTE.

BOLIVIA

THE BAR'S RICH NOTES OF BLACK TRUFFLE AND WALNUT ARE EXCELLENT, WITH A HINT OF SOUR CHERRY.

DOMINICAN + NIBS

THE POINTED RED CURRANT FLAVOUR IMMEDIATELY HITS THE PALATE, FOLLOWED BY A CRUNCHY NUTTINESS OF THE ROASTED NIBS SPRINKLED ON THE BAR.

ECUADOR

THE RICH ECUADORIAN CACAO EMULATES TRANQUILITY, WITH NOTES OF HONEY AND JASMINE GRACING THIS SWEET CHOCOLATE.

GUATEMALA

THIS FRUITY CHOCOLATE BEGINS WITH THE FAMILIAR NOTE OF SOUR GRAPES AND JOURNEYS THROUGH SWEET FLORAL NOTES AND ENDS ON A SWEET SHORTBREAD NOTE.

VINTAGE PLANTATIONS

— SWEDEN —

Vintage Plantations dates from the late 1990s when French chocolatier Pierrick Chouard was inspired by a visit to a cacao farm in the Dominican Republic. Since then the business has vastly expanded and there are numerous strategic partners on a global scale. The Swedish division is owned by Pierrick Chouard, Jenny Berg and Lars Stenbom. This creative team has experimented with several unusual flavour combinations, like incorporating locally grown native berries and herbs (foraged from the woods), as well as producing some extraordinary single-origin bars. The specially commissioned colourful artwork on the packaging is a true delight.

The surprisingly addictive salty liquorice chocolate is mind-blowing.

LIQUORICE

SUPER SALTY PIECES OF SWEDISH LIQUORICE AND GROUND LIQUORICE
ROOT COMBINED WITH DARK CHOCOLATE PROVIDES THE PERFECT MATCH
BETWEEN SWEET AND SALTY.

65%
WELL-BALANCED TANNINS WITH A HAZELNUT CREAMY TASTE AT FIRST, FOLLOWED BY MOLASSES, CARAMEL AND SOME COCONUT FLAVOURS. IT HAS A LONG PLEASANT AFTERTASTE OF LIQUORICE.

85%
THIS CONTAINS A MILD CACAO FLAVOUR WHILE THE STONE-GROUND BEANS BESTOW A RUSTIC TEXTURE, AND HAS EARTHY NOTES WITH A HINT OF HAZEL NUTS, CARAMEL AND GREEN TEA.

ANGELICA
ANGELICA SEEDS COMBINED WITH THE DARK CHOCOLATE GIVE A HINT OF ANISE, ORANGE, FENNEL AND SOME FRESH MINT AT THE END.

BLACKCURRANT

WELL-BALANCED DARK CHOCOLATE
WITH SWEDISH BLACKCURRANT THAT
PROVIDES A SWEET AND FRUITY FLAVOUR
WITH GOOD ACIDITY.

CRANBERRY

MILDLY ACIDIC DARK CHOCOLATE MIXED
WITH TART CRANBERRIES, THIS IS FRUITY
AND SPICY AT THE SAME TIME WITH LONG
PLEASANT FLAVOUR NOTES.

NIBS

WELL-BALANCED TANNINS WITH A
FLORAL TASTE AT FIRST, FOLLOWED BY
MOLASSES, CARAMEL AND SOME COCONUT
FLAVOURS. LONG PLEASANT AFTERTASTE
WITH NO BITTERNESS.

WELLINGTON CHOCOLATE FACTORY

— NEW ZEALAND —

Wellington Chocolate Factory is situated right in the heart of New Zealand's vibrant capital city. The company has developed sustainable working relationships with farmers across the globe. All of its bars are handmade (on traditional machinery) from the finest cacao beans in small batches to ensure optimum quality. It also practices traditional manufacturing techniques (dating back to the eighteenth century). This ensures all of its small-batch bean-to-bar chocolate has an intense taste. The brand employs renowned New Zealand artists to design its gorgeous bright packaging.

There are so many tempting flavours to choose from but the scrumptious Chilli Lime Nuts is a winner.

✽ · ✽ · ✽ · ✽ · ✽

CHILLI LIME NUTS

PEANUTS CARAMELISED IN HONEY AND A TRINITY OF GINGER, MAKRUT
LIME LEAVES AND RED CHILLIES CREATE DEPTH AS WELL AS HEAT.

BOUGAINVILLE BAR

MADE USING SINGLE-ORIGIN CACAO FROM BOUGAINVILLE, PAPUA NEW GUINEA, THIS BAR IS ASTRINGENT WITH NOTES OF PORT AND RAISINS, AND SLIGHT HINTS OF TROPICAL FRUIT.

THE GREAT WAR B

CREAMY COCONUT-M
CHOCOLATE IS TOPP
WITH CRUNCHY HOU
MADE ANZAC OAT BIS
TO CREATE A SWEET
VEGAN TREAT.

NEW ZEALAND HAZELNUTS

A HOUSE BLEND OF CRIOLLO AND TRINITARIO CHOCOLATE IS TOPPED WITH A DENSE COVERING OF LIGHTLY TOASTED AND CRUSHED NEW ZEALAND HAZELNUTS, GIVING A CRUNCHY TEXTURE.

SAMOA BAR

MADE USING SINGLE-ORIGIN CACAO FROM
SAMOA, THE BEANS ARE NATURALLY IMBUED BY
THE CROPS THAT SURROUND IT, RESULTING IN
NOTES OF BANANA AND TOBACCO.

SALTED BRITTLE CARAMEL

HOUSE-MADE BRITTLE CARAMEL
CHUNKS PLUNGED INTO BARS
OF CHOCOLATE AND TOPPED OFF
WITH DELICATE SEA SALT, FOR A
CONTRASTING TASTE EXPLOSION
AND A CRUNCHY TEXTURE.

WILD HEART CHOCOLATE

— NEW ZEALAND —

Wild Heart Chocolate is based in Auckland, New Zealand's largest city, and was founded by Chalice Malcom who promotes health and well-being, and is also a Shamanic practitioner. What makes its raw bars special is the way the cacao beans are harvested (in contrast to more commercial methods). The company only ethically sources the highest quality wild-grown cacao beans directly from indigenous gatherers in the Amazon. This supports the indigenous people and also the preservation of the Amazon forest. It also means that the chocolate has a more intense and robust flavour, as well as being sensationally rich with a creamy intensity. This is a chocolate you will relish, and the complex taste notes are incredible.

The creamy Zest bar is both refreshing and rich, combining citrus with a hint of warm spice notes.

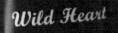

Wild Heart

Raw Organic
Chocolate

ZEST

ZEST

ORGANIC TREE-RIPENED
ORANGE ZEST ADDS A TASTE
OF SUMMER TO THIS CREAMY
ORANGE CHOCOLATE DELIGHT.
WITH A HINT OF ANISE AND
CARDAMOM.

GOJI

NOURISHING AND SWEET, THE ACTIVATED ALMONDS ADD A
GROUNDING CRUNCH TO THE SWEETNESS OF THE GOJI.

BERRYLION

WILD CACAO, MIXED WITH THE SWEET FLAVOURS
OF RASPBERRIES AND BLUEBERRIES, PROVES TO BE A
DELIGHTFUL TREAT, FULL OF ANTIOXIDANTS.

RAW LOVE

RICH DARK CRUNCHY, WILD RAW CACAO GOODNESS.

BLISS
A CREAMY SOFT MELT-IN-YOUR-MOUTH EXPERIENCE,
WITH INDIAN CINNAMON AND SWEET TONGAN VANILLA.

WILD HEART CHOCOLATE IS AN ADVENTURE INTO THE HEART AND OUR CONNECTION TO THIS WORLD. THE POWERFUL GIFT RAW CACAO GIVES US IS TO EXPERIENCE THE LOVE THAT IS THERE; IT OPENS US. IT'S IMPORTANT TO US TO KNOW WHERE OUR INGREDIENTS COME FROM AND WHERE THEY ARE GOING TO. LIFE IS ABOUT CONNECTIONS AND RELATIONSHIPS.

Chalice Malcolm, FOUNDER, WILD HEART CHOCOLATE

MINT SONG
CRISP MINT ESSENCE INTERTWINED WITH THE CRUNCH OF
RAW NIBS AND THE INTEGRITY OF WILD CACAO.

WILDNESS CHOCOLATE

— NEW ZEALAND —

As a trained chef and chocolatier in Wellington, New Zealand, Marie Monmont is always experimenting with different flavour combinations. After a visit to Brazil several years ago she discovered a fruit called *cupuaçu,* which has a creamy dense texture and is related to cacao. By combining this with cacao and other delicious ingredients she has created a superior range of vegan chocolate bars. Even though this chocolate is dairy-free, the cocoa content isn't that high (65%), giving it a seductive smooth and creamy texture.

Try the moreish Walnuts bar for a truly rich and luxurious sensation.

ORGANIC
WILDNESS
Chocolate

57% COCOA
DARK CHOCOLATE
with WALNUTS

70g

WALNUTS
DRY ON THE PALATE, THE RICHNESS
OF THE CACAO MIXES WELL WITH THE
WOODY FLAVOUR OF THE WALNUT.

ORGANIC
WILDNESS
Chocolate

RICH
DARK
CHOCOLATE

NEW ZEALAND

CUPUAÇU AND CASHEWS

CRISPY ROASTED CASHEW NUTS
ARE MIXED WITH THE TROPICAL
CUPUAÇU, AND ENVELOPED
TOGETHER IN THE SMOOTHNESS OF
THE DARK CACAO.

AÇAI DIPPED IN CUPUAÇU

THE BERRYLIKE AÇAI HAS A TART FLAVOUR, WHICH COMBINES WONDERFULLY WITH THE CHOCOLATE. THE *CUPUAÇU* BRINGS A SWEET TASTE ON THE PALATE TO EASE THE DEGUSTATION.

CUPUAÇU

THE *CUPUAÇU*, WHICH TASTES LIKE A CARAMELISED PEAR AT THE START, HAS A TANGY FINISH. THE SMOOTH CHOCOLATE BRINGS OUT HINTS OF AÇAI, BLACK PEPPER AND CARDAMOM.

CUPUAÇU AND COCONUT

THE DELICATE AND TROPICAL TASTE OF COCONUT ENGAGES WITH THE TANGY *CUPUAÇU* COVERED WITH PURE DARK SILK CHOCOLATE.

57%

THIS IS A RICH, DARK EXPERIENCE ON THE PALATE, WITH A STRONG CHOCOLATE TASTE AND OVERALL SMOOTHNESS. THE FINISHING IS A LIGHT SWEET EARTHY FLAVOUR.

CREDITS

All brand images are supplied courtesy of the company, unless otherwise noted. See also photography credits on page 208.

Alter Eco 38–41
alterecofoods.com
altereco.com.au
San Francisco, CA, USA

AMMA Chocolate 42–45
ammachocolate.com.br
Sao Paulo, Brazil

Antidote Chocolate 46–49
antidotechoco.com
New York, NY, USA
Photography: Ailin Blasco

Bahen & Co 50–53
bahenchocolate.com
Margaret River, WA, Australia

Cacaoken 54–57
cacaoken.com
Fukuoka, Japan

Caoni Chocolate 58–61
caonichocolate.com
Quito, Ecuador

Chaleur B Chocolat 62–65
chaleurb.com
Carleton, Quebec, Canada
Photography: Benoit Daoust

Chocolat Madagascar 66–69
chocolatmadagascar.com
Antananarivo, Madagascar
Photography: Kristen Malone

Chow Cacao 70–73
chowcacao.com.au
Byron Bay, NSW, Australia

Claudio Corallo 74–77
claudiocorallo.com
São Tomé, São Tomé and
Príncipe

Clonakilty Chocolate 78–81
clonakiltychocolate.com
Clonakilty, Ireland

Conscious Chocolate 82–85
consciouschocolate.com
Small Dole, UK

Earth Loaf 86–89
earthloaf.co.in
Mysore, India
Photography: David Belo

Equal Exchange 90–93
equalexchange.coop
West Bridgewater, MA, USA

Fu Wan Chocolate 94–97
fuwanshop.com
Donggang Township, Taiwan
Photography: Warren Hsu

Goodnow Farms Chocolate 98–101
goodnowfarms.com
Sudbury, MA, USA

Green & Black's 102–5
greenandblacks.co.uk
London, UK

Jasper & Myrtle 106–9
jasperandmyrtle.com.au
Canberra, ACT, Australia

Made with Raw Love 110–13
madewithrawlove.com
Northern Rivers, NSW, Australia
Photography: Lucia Ondrosuva

Malagos Chocolate 114–17
malagoschocolate.com
Davao City, Philippines
Photography: Jason Quibilan

Mamuschka 118–21
mamuschka.com
Bariloche, Argentina

Marsatta Chocolate 122–25
marsatta.com
Torrance, CA, USA
Photography: Bev Baigent
Photography

Mashpi Chocolate Artesanal 126–29
chocomashpi.com
Pichincha, Ecuador

Mason & Co 130–33
masonchocolate.com
Kuilapalayam, India
Photography: Natasha Mulhall
Photography; Nayantara Parikh

Monsieur Truffe 134–37
monsieurtruffechocolate.com
Melbourne, VIC, Australia
Photography: Elizabeth Berry;
Jessica Field

Nahua Chocolate 138–41
nahuachocolate.com
Cariari, Costa Rica
Photography: María Fernanda
Arias

OCHO 142–45
ocho.co.nz
Dunedin, New Zealand

Origin Chocolate 146–49
originchocolate.com.au
Orange, NSW, Australia

Pod Chocolate 150–53
podchocolate.com
Bali, Indonesia

Ranger Chocolate Company 154–57
rangerchocolate.com
Portland, OR, USA
Photography: Kristen Manning
Photography

RAWR 158–61
rawrchoc.com
Gainsborough, UK
Photography: Mr O. Blumenfeld

Seatonfire Chilli Chocolate 162–65
seatonfire.com
Murphys Creek, QLD, Australia

She Universe 166–69
sheuniverse.com
Christchurch, New Zealand
Photography: Osho Prior

Solstice Chocolate 170–73
solsticechocolate.com
Murray, UT, USA
Photography: Christiana Huish

Stone Grindz Chocolate 174–77
stonegrindz.com
Scottsdale, AZ, USA

Tabal Chocolate 178–81
tabalchocolate.com
Wauwatosa, WI, USA
Photography: Dan Bieser

Tonantzin Chocolate 182–85
tonantzinchocolate.com
Yarra Junction, VIC, Australia
Photography: Kate Baker

Vicuña Chocolate 186–89
vicunachocolate.com
Peterborough, NH, USA
Photography: Casey Goodrich

Vintage Plantations 190–93
vintageplantations.com
Umeå, Sweden
Photography: Per Lundberg,
Lumorfoto

Wellington Chocolate Factory 194–97
wcf.co.nz
Wellington, New Zealand
Photography: Inject Design

Wild Heart Chocolate 198–201
wildheartchocolate.co.nz
Auckland, New Zealand

Wildness Chocolate 202–5
wildness.co.nz
Wellington, New Zealand

Published in Australia in 2019 by Peleus Press, an imprint of
The Images Publishing Group Pty Ltd
ABN 89 059 734 431

Offices

Australia
6 Bastow Place
Mulgrave, Victoria 3170
Australia
Tel: +61 3 9561 5544

United States
6 West 18th Street 4B
New York, NY 10011
United States
Tel: +1 212 645 1111

books@imagespublishing.com
www.imagespublishing.com

A catalogue record for this
book is available from the
National Library of Australia

Title: Dark Chocolate: A Guide to Artisan Chocolatiers / by Steve Huyton
ISBN: 9781864708066

This title was commissioned in IMAGES' Melbourne office and produced as follows: *Editorial coordination* Jeanette Wall,
Graphic design & production Nicole Boehringer, *Senior editorial* Gina Tsarouhas

Printed on 140gsm Sun Woodfree paper by Everbest Printing Investment Limited, in Hong Kong/China